LOST BOY

LOST BOY

BRENT W. JEFFS

with Maia Szalavitz

BROADWAY BOOKS / NEW YORK

Copyright © 2009 by Brent Jeffs and Maia Szalavitz

All Rights Reserved

Published in the United States by Broadway Books, an imprint of the Crown
Publishing Group, a division of Random House, Inc., New York.

www.broadwaybooks.com

BROADWAY BOOKS and its logo, a letter B bisected on the diagonal, are trademarks of
Random House, Inc.

Photo credits appear on page 243.

Book design by Casey Hampton

LIBRARY OF CONGRESS CATALOGING-IN-PUBLICATION DATA
Jeffs, Brent W.
Lost boy / by Brent W. Jeffs with Maia Szalavitz.
p. cm.
Includes bibliographical references.
1. Jeffs, Brent W. 2. Polygamy—United States. 3. Mormons—United States—Biography.
4. Sexual abuse—United States. 5. Mormon fundamentalism—United States.
6. Fundamentalist Church of Jesus Christ of Latter Day Saints. I. Szalavitz, Maia. II. Title.
HQ994.J44 2009
289.3092—dc22
[B]
2008053028

ISBN 978-0-7679-3177-9

PRINTED IN THE UNITED STATES OF AMERICA

1 3 5 7 9 10 8 6 4 2

FIRST EDITION

For Clayne and David

Contents

AUTHOR'S NOTE

This is my true story, based on my memories and the recollections of people close to me. Memory is never perfect, but I have done my best to accurately portray the unique world that shaped me. Some names have been changed to protect privacy.

LOST BOY

Prologue

I woke up drenched in sweat, screaming. My heart felt like it was going to burst out of my chest, my throat was dry and raw as sand. Jody—my then-fiancée, now wife—was trying to calm me. She was holding me, rocking me, gently touching my hair. "It's okay, it's okay, it's only a dream," she said. I was safe in my bed, at home in the Salt Lake suburb of Bluffdale, wrapped up in the black and yellow leopard-patterned comforter I'd kept from my bachelor days. Jody was with me.

But in my mind, I was back at Alta Academy—the private religious school run by my uncle, Warren Jeffs. Warren is now the prophet of the Fundamentalist Church of Jesus Christ of Latter Day Saints (FLDS), a Mormon splinter sect of about ten thousand people who believe that the church erred when it abandoned polygamy. Back then, he was the principal of my school. My dad, his three wives, and all twenty of us children had been born into the church.

In my dream, Warren was holding my hand. His hand seemed huge and mine was tiny. He's 6' 4", gawky, scrawny, and awkward—his neck is too skinny for his head and his glasses are too big for his face. His hair and eyes are a muddy brown. It seemed to me like the rest of him was really far way, like his hand came down toward mine from an incredible height.

I was in a small, cramped classroom. The kids around me were little ones, preschoolers and kindergartners, my youngest cousins. That meant it must have been a Sunday, during Jeffs family church. My dad has more than sixty-five brothers and sisters—his father had about nineteen wives at that time. Every other Sunday, our whole family would have our own special services led by my grandfather, who was then the prophet.

To keep the little kids occupied while the adults worshipped, we were sent into classrooms in the basement and allowed to play, watched over by teenage sisters or cousins who had been assigned babysitting duty. That's where I was when Warren tapped my shoulder and grabbed my hand.

I followed him, like you do when an uncle takes your hand and you are five. He took me into the hallway, which was paneled in dark wood and narrow. There were many doors along that corridor. One opened. I saw a flash of a bathroom with some pale blue tiles.

And then, terror. Jody says I was screaming in my sleep: "No, stop, please. Don't touch me." She tried to wake me but couldn't immediately. All I remember feeling was overwhelming panic, pain, and helplessness. Something terrible was going to happen to me, something horrendous and unstoppable.

I was small and powerless and couldn't do anything about it. And it would hurt: beyond words. I knew this with complete certainty—because, I realized, whatever it was, it had happened to me before. Now I dreaded it more than anything, even death. I felt frozen, just blank with fear and powerlessness.

As I began to wake up, I thought my body had been paralyzed. I tried to scream, tried to move my arms, legs, fingers, toes—but nothing worked. Not a sound seemed to come from my mouth and my limbs wouldn't move. I knew the pain would take over soon. I was unable to protect myself. Every single part of me was electrified by terror and apprehension.

I jumped. Jody had snapped me out of it, and now I saw her and realized where I was. My heart was still speeding, but it began to slow. I didn't know—or really, I didn't want to know—what had just terrorized me. I'd been having similar nightmares for months. They seemed so real. I didn't want to think about why.

I did know that my brother Clayne had been raped by Warren at Alta Academy—when he was about five years old. That made me flash on an image of Clayne's body after he'd shot himself—another thing I was trying to forget. It had been more than a year ago now, but I still felt like it had just happened and still didn't want to believe it was true. Asleep, I sometimes managed to forget my grief.

Now I was beginning to think that the abuse that had driven my oldest brother to suicide was something I'd have to confront as well. I started thinking back to what had happened when I'd left the church—and how I'd gotten to the point that I had to leave. I thought of my life as a "lost boy." That's what the media came to call the hundreds of young men like me who had been forced out of the church to provide more young women for Warren and his followers. I thought about how that life had affected my brothers.

And, as I sifted through my memories, my life came to me in bits and pieces, often disconnected, just like my dreams. Even normal memory has gaps, but traumatic memory is even more discontinuous. This is my story, which put me back together.

PART ONE

Heaven or Hell

Every child believes he's special. But when you are number ten of twenty, with three "sister-mothers"—two of whom are full-blooded sisters—and a grandfather whom thousands of people believe speaks directly to God, it can be hard to figure out what "special" really means.

All told, I have roughly sixty-five aunts and uncles on my dad's side and twenty-two on my mom's—with probably thousands of cousins. In families as large as mine, even keeping track of your own siblings—let alone cousins and aunts and uncles—is difficult.

As a grandson of Rulon Jeffs and nephew of Warren Jeffs, it once seemed that I was destined for high honor in the FLDS. My family had what our church called "royal blood." We were direct descendants of our prophet through my father's line. My mother, too, is the child of a prophet, who split from our group in 1978 to lead his own polygamous sect.

When I was little, my family was favored, in the church's elite. I was assured that there was a place for me in the highest realms of heaven and at least three wives for me right here on earth once I attained the

Melchizedek priesthood. I was in a chosen family in a chosen people, visiting sacred land near end times. I would one day become a god, ruling over my own spinning world.

So why would I ever abandon such status and rank? In the world of the FLDS, things are not always what they seem. The shiny, smiling surfaces often hide a world of rot and pain. And even royal blood and being born male can't protect you from sudden changes in its convoluted power structure.

Outsiders tend to think our form of polygamy must be a great deal for us men. You get sexual variety without guilt: in fact, you are commanded by God to have multiple partners and the women are expected to go along with it. Indeed, they are supposed to be happy about doing so and obediently serve you. This is the only way for all of you to get to the highest realms of heaven.

To many men, that sounds like heaven right there, without any need for the afterlife part. They focus on the sex—fantasizing about a harem of young, beautiful women, all at their beck and call. They don't think about the responsibility—or the balancing act needed to keep all of those women happy, or even just to minimize their complaints. During the one full year I attended public school, the few guys who befriended me rather than ridiculing me were fascinated by it all.

But while it might seem good in theory, in practice, at least in my experience, it's actually a recipe for misery for everyone involved. In the FLDS anyway, polygamy and its power structure continuously produce a constant, exhausting struggle for attention and resources.

In families as large as mine, it simply isn't possible for all of the women and children to get their needs met. Just making sure the children are fed, clothed, and physically accounted for is an ongoing challenge. Simply keeping dozens of children physically safe is close to impossible.

I'd estimate that maybe one in five FLDS families has lost a child early in life, frequently from accidents that better supervision could have prevented. And that number doesn't include deaths related to the genetic disorder that runs in our church—which handicaps and often kills children very early in life but which many members refuse to see as a result of marriages among closely related families.

For the father, even though he's at the top of the heap in his own family, he must constantly disappoint, reject, ignore, and/or fail to satisfy at least some wives and kids. There's only so much of his time and attention to go around, and supporting such a large family takes many hours, too. At home, if one person has your ear, someone else doesn't. Yes to one wife is no to the others. And, if a man wants more wives, he will have to engage in his own highly competitive fight for status and influence with the higher-ups in the church.

Then there's the math problem: half of all children born are boys, of course. For some men to have many wives, others are either going to have to leave, recruit new women into polygamy (a difficult task, unsurprisingly—and one rarely attempted by the FLDS), or go unmarried.

Consequently, being born a boy in the FLDS is not the privileged position it first seems to be. Unless you are willing to kowtow to the leaders and attempt perfect obedience with constantly changing demands and hierarchies, you are likely either to be expelled or to have a hard time getting even one wife, let alone the required three. Just on the numbers alone, you will need a lot of luck to avoid losing everything as you hit manhood. Being born into the right family like I was is a good start—however, it may not be enough.

Once people get over their titillation and harem fantasies, and think through these issues, they start wondering why anyone stays. "How can you believe such strange things?" they ask. "Why didn't you leave years earlier?" "And how could those parents marry their teenage daughters off to old men, abandon their sons, or give up their wives and children at Warren's command?"

The answer is tangled in family loyalties, family history, and a church that has become expert at using these bonds to move beliefs into brainwashing.

On my father's side, I come from around six generations of polygamy. My mother's history is similar. Our families have lived polygamy since Joseph Smith first introduced "the principle" of "celestial marriage" in 1843—and the same is true for most members. One reason we stay is that this is the only life we know. Another is that leaving involves giving up contact with basically every single family member and friend you have—sometimes, everyone you know, period.

And, too, there's the fact that you have been kept ignorant of the way the rest of the world works: you have been indoctrinated nearly every single day of your life to believe that all other peoples are evil, wish to harm you, and are damned by God, unchosen.

It's weird, but even if you truly don't believe what they have told you, some part of you remains frightened that they may be right and that fear—and your fear of losing everyone you love—is at the heart of what traps people. Then there's the weight of family history and tradition.

My great-grandfather, David W. Jeffs, was born in 1873 and baptized in the Mormon Church when polygamy was officially part of the religion. Founder Joseph Smith had begun practicing polygamy before he preached it. The identity of his second wife is disputed because the ceremony took place in secret, without even the knowledge of his first wife, who vigorously opposed the whole idea.

As Smith's biographer Fawn Brodie wrote, Joseph Smith "believed in the good life . . . 'Man is that he might have joy' had been one of his first significant pronouncements in the Book of Mormon."[1] The prophet's belief in the rightness of things that gave him joy meant that he couldn't see having more than one wife as sinful. That just didn't make sense to him. Of course, a prophet couldn't have mistresses. And so, "celestial marriage" was born. It is not known how many wives Joseph Smith had—but the number is believed to be around fifty.

Joseph Smith's revelation on plural wives was grounded in the Old Testament, and in our church it is sometimes called the Law of Sarah, who was Abraham's first wife. The Jewish patriarchs and kings of the Old Testament were polygamous. While the rest of Christianity accepts the New Testament and rejects polygamy, fundamentalist Mormons believe that the Book of Mormon supersedes the New Testament in the way that the New Testament updates the Old.

Joseph Smith's 1843 revelation on polygamy was personally directed at his resistant first wife. He was tired of hiding his other wives from her and everyone else and wanted it all out in the open. He wrote that God told him, "I command mine handmaid, Emma Smith," to "receive all those that have been given unto my servant Joseph" and "cleave unto my servant Joseph and to none else . . . if she will not abide this commandment she shall be destroyed."[2]

Believing this to be a true revelation, Emma complied. Still, she didn't hesitate to expel from her home the women she believed her husband was favoring—and, according to some, she once demanded her own "spiritual husbands" as fair play. Needless to say, a revelation making this practice into gospel was never received by Joseph Smith.

The rest of the doctrine on plural marriage is written this way: "If any man espouse a virgin, and desire to espouse another, and the first give her consent, and if he espouse the second, and they are virgins, and have vowed to no other man, then is he justified; he cannot commit adultery . . . and if he have ten virgins given unto him by this law, he cannot commit adultery, for they belong to him."[3] Given Emma's strenuous objections, clearly, Joseph Smith had a very flexible definition of consent. Unfortunately, that probably had a great influence on the fundamentalist church.

And oddly, despite the prohibition against marrying those who "have vowed to another man," many of the first Mormon plural wives also had other husbands. Some had left their spouses to join the church and were essentially separated. But others were married first to other Mormon men, then to leaders like Joseph Smith who decided that they wanted those particular women for themselves. Being lower in the church hierarchy, many men accepted this—some even saw it as an honor.

Probably for public relations purposes, the marriages of church leaders to women with other husbands were originally presented as unions that were "for eternity," but not "for time." In other words, they weren't supposed to involve sex here on earth. However, accounts of the time suggest that these marriages were consummated and indeed sometimes produced children. In the FLDS, when a polygamous marriage is entered into, it is "sealed" by the prophet both "for time" and "for eternity."

My former church doesn't just preach multiple wives, however; it also preaches multiple gods and multiple heavens. Understanding this is important to understanding what happened to my family and how the FLDS works.

Joseph Smith preached that "God himself was once as we are now," and Lorenzo Snow, the fifth president of the LDS church, wrote, "As man is, God once was; and as God is, man may become."[4] That's a very exciting idea for many people—and you can see why it might have helped the early church attract converts. But by the 1860s, this transformation from man to God began to require the practice of polygamy.

As Brigham Young proclaimed, "The only men who become Gods, even the Sons of God, are those who enter into polygamy. Others attain unto a glory . . . but they cannot reign as kings in glory, because they had blessing offered unto them, and they refused to accept them."[5]

The idea that one should never reject a blessing is a cornerstone of the FLDS belief system—one that would also have a profound impact on my family and my life. As you'll see, there were several "blessings" that we truly could have lived without. But my parents didn't feel that they could reject them. Few people in the church felt they could challenge this doctrine. That would mean failing at another key objective in the church: being obedient.

The FLDS conception of heaven is complicated, too. In our religion, it's not getting into heaven that counts—it's getting into the right heaven. There are three realms. The highest and most "glorious" is the "celestial," which can be entered only by men who have had at least three wives in polygamy. Here, men become godlike and rule over their own planets. The reason that FLDS members have so many children, in fact, is to populate their personal planets.

In the celestial realm, plural wives become "queens," who bear celestial children (yeah, women get a raw deal even in the highest realm of heaven in our religion). The middle realm is the "terrestrial"—this is somewhat like purgatory in Catholicism and is for people who never knew the teachings of Joseph Smith and Jesus Christ, but it's still supposed to be pretty glorious.

The lowest realm is the "telestial," which is for people who refused to worship God. This is not hell, it's just a kind of mediocre heaven. Hell is reserved for the worst of sinners who refuse to repent and continue to wallow in sin. They are called the Sons or Daughters of Perdition.

Not surprisingly, as word of Mormon views on polygamy and men becoming gods first became public, the Gentile world was shocked and outraged. At the time of Joseph Smith's polygamy revelation, Mormons had already fled both Ohio and Missouri (in the case of Missouri, it was under threat of extermination by the governor).

It was non-Mormon fury over polygamy and over Joseph Smith's growing political power that led to his assassination in 1844 in an Illinois jail and to the subsequent migration to Utah led by Brigham Young. The main LDS church banned polygamy in 1890 to pave the way for Utah statehood, which was granted in 1896. The manifesto that prohibited plural marriage made clear that the ban was being imposed only because the practice was illegal and the U.S. Supreme Court had ruled that laws against it were constitutional. But the LDS didn't begin excommunicating polygamists until 1904.

I don't know when my father's family converted to Mormonism. But when the polygamy ban took effect, my great-grandfather David W. Jeffs had already married plural wives in the church and refused to give them up. He sided with the men who would become the first leaders of the FLDS. They believed that the Mormon leaders who accepted the end of polygamy were not the true holders of the keys to the holy priesthood preached by Smith. These keys are important because, in Mormon belief, only those who have been given them by a legitimate authority can truly be prophets. Without them, prophets have no authority and men cannot receive true revelations. Lines of patriarchal authority— through these keys and through blood—shape most aspects of life in the fundamentalist church.

My great-grandfather believed that these sacred keys had been passed to the FLDS leadership, during an event known as the "eight-hour meeting." This occurred in 1886. At that time, John Taylor was the president and prophet of the whole LDS church. He was living underground, to avoid federal prosecution for polygamy.

Lorrin Woolley, who would become a prophet of the FLDS, guarded the door to the room where Taylor was staying the night before the meeting. He said that it had no door to the outside of the house and had covered windows. According to his account, "I was suddenly attracted to a light appearing under the door leading to President Taylor's room and was at once startled to hear the voices of men talking there. I was bewildered because it was my duty to keep people out of that room and evidently someone had entered without my knowing it."[6]

Woolley said that Taylor told him the next day that the voices he had heard had been those of "your Lord" and Joseph Smith, and that they had instructed him not to sign a manifesto banning polygamy. Woolley wrote that at the eight-hour meeting Taylor "placed his finger on the document, his person rising from the floor about a foot or 18 inches," and said that he would sooner have his tongue or arm cut off than sign it.[7]

He then gave five men who were at the meeting (including Woolley) the right to perform polygamous marriages. He made them swear that they would ensure that "no year passed by without children being born in the principle of plural marriage."[8]

The first two prophets of the FLDS church were among the five selected to carry out these marriages. But while great-grandfather David Jeffs sided with the fundamentalists, my grandfather Rulon, who was born in 1909, became opposed to polygamy as a young man. He was baptized into the LDS and became estranged from his fundamentalist father.

Tall and handsome in his youth, Rulon had mischievous brown eyes and chestnut brown hair, although his hairline started receding quite early. He trained as an accountant, and after a mission to England during the Great Depression, he took a job in Salt Lake City with the Utah State Tax Commission. Clearly seen as a man of promise by the LDS, my grandfather Rulon was permitted to marry Zola Brown, the daughter of one of the highest-ranking leaders of the church, known as an apostle.

After he had his first son, however, Rulon reconnected with his father. David soon convinced him that he should live polygamy. But Rulon ran into the same problems with his first wife that Joseph Smith had had. She did not want to share him. Although Rulon built their new home with basement accommodations for a second wife, unlike Emma Smith, Zola Jeffs utterly refused to submit.

When Rulon told her in July 1940 that a mountaintop revelation had shown him that God had designated a cute young shop clerk in Provo to be his second wife, Zola broke down. According to their divorce papers, she became "so worried and upset that she cried almost day and night, that her milk dried up so she was no longer able to nurse her baby."[9] She took the couple's two small children and moved to California. Two weeks after a judge granted the divorce in 1941, Rulon was excommunicated by the LDS.

My grandfather, however, was not to be deterred. He didn't even go to his own LDS church trial. He wrote, "For the first time I say, I would put God's work before anything else in my life."[10] He joined a group led by John Y. Barlow, who was the FLDS* prophet from 1935 to 1949. In 1986, Grandfather Rulon would himself become the prophet.

And that put my family right at the center of an organization that was extremely loyal to its leaders. The church reflected and amplified both its leader's good sides and his flaws. With a relaxed leadership, the FLDS was mighty peculiar, but not particularly perverse. There was child abuse and domestic violence in some families, but there is no way of knowing whether abuse was more common in our church than anywhere else at the time. The problem was the FLDS's growing isolation—and a change in leadership structure that would inevitably produce corruption.

Before my grandfather came to power, there had been a leadership council that ran the church. This council was more powerful than most religious hierarchies because—at least in Colorado City and Hildale, where two thirds of the FLDS lived at the time—most people's houses were owned by the church, not by the people who lived in them. This occurred through a system that became known as the United Effort Plan (UEP). The communal arrangement was based on one used by the early Mormons.

The council provided at least some checks on the prophet's control over the group. It ensured that he did not have absolute power over both theology and property. But part of what brought Grandfather to the prophet's position was his opposition to that council—and his belief in what they called "one man rule."

A dispute over this issue splintered the FLDS in the late 1970s and early 1980s. My grandfather's position swayed the majority, who stayed, with the belief that the prophet should have absolute power. Rulon would eventually have this power for himself. And this set the stage for his son Warren, who would use the idea that he was God's special messenger to do unspeakable evil, without any voice of reason or earthly authority to stop him.

---

* The FLDS did not formally incorporate under that name until some time in the 1940s. Prior to that it had just been known as "The Work," but I will use the term they are now known by throughout for clarity.

Weddings and War

Leroy Johnson's office was a lot like his style as a prophet: plain, folksy, and not at all flashy. It was a small converted bedroom with one little window, located on the third floor of a turn-of-the-century Salt Lake City home on Lincoln Street. The prophet sat in a swivel chair, near a rolltop desk, with a couch and some other chairs for visitors. His main home was in Colorado City, but after a 1953 raid on polygamists, church members had scattered to avoid further scrutiny.

It was 1968—and my mom, Susan, had come to see Uncle Roy to "present herself" for marriage. In our church, the prophet is always called "Uncle" as a term of respect and connection. To understand my story, you have to understand how marriage worked in the church at that time—and my father's unique situation as the only one of Rulon's dozens of sons to serve in the Vietnam War.

Susan was eighteen that year, the year after the summer of love, when hippies in New York and San Francisco were dropping acid and questioning authority. But her concerns were far away from all that. For her, authority was holy.

She was deeply religious, having taken the precepts of faith that she was taught as a child straight to heart. Her green eyes were kind and I'm sure she looked beautiful, dressed in her Sunday best. She wore a long, chaste dress, her luxuriant brown hair tucked up in a bun. Mom had been raised in a polygamous family in Salt Lake City, with two sister-mothers and nearly two dozen siblings.

There hadn't been much noticeable strife between her moms. They lived in separate houses and their father split his time between these two homes. For almost all of her childhood, Uncle Roy had been the prophet. He had ascended when Susan was just four years old.

Mom had long dreamed of her wedding day and her entry into celestial marriage. She was prepared for anything: if her path was to be a second, fourth, or tenth wife to an older man or a first wife to a young one, it was up to God and she understood and accepted that. Via the prophet's revelations, she would discover God's will for her, and she was devoutly determined to be as obedient as she possibly could. Her life was focused on following the church's command to "keep sweet." This meant submitting to its rules and leader and through him, God, not grudgingly but happily.

Susan had already had a good deal of practice at keeping sweet. Throughout her childhood, she always wanted to be a "good girl" and worked hard at it. Though she remembers that her sisters and brothers were whipped with a thin willow branch from time to time when they acted up, she was usually well behaved and doesn't even recall being spanked.

In her family, she was the oldest girl of her mom's seventeen children. Her father's second wife had twelve. Seven of those children, tragically, suffered from a genetic disorder that runs in the FLDS called fumarase deficiency and didn't live to adulthood. At the time, not much was known about it and Mom's parents didn't see it as genetic. The defect is caused by a problem with a chemical needed to give energy to the body and brain. Sadly, it is usually fatal in early childhood, stunting brain development and causing seizures and wide-ranging disability.[1]

Three children with fumarase deficiency were born to my blood grandmother. And so, in my mom's household, one brother with the disorder died at five, a sister died at seven, and another brother lived until fifteen. My mom helped take care of all of them, but especially the oldest boy. His bed was in her room until she left home to get married, and then some of her younger sisters took over his care.

Mom's family saw these children as a blessing from God, believing that they had been sent from heaven so that the family could learn and grow by caring for them. Under Warren, children with this same birth defect would later be seen as a curse, a sign of sin. But under Uncle Roy, Mom's family didn't have to live with that added burden.

And so, long before she became a mom herself, she was changing diapers, rubbing the sick children's painfully underdeveloped arms and legs, making sure they were breathing, and feeding and otherwise caring for them. They were like babies who didn't grow up. They taught her compassion, Mom says. And, although the affected siblings couldn't walk or talk, they could laugh.

Mom remembers them fondly for their beautiful eyes, curly eyelashes, and those smiles and laughter. Of course, caring for them was also a tremendous challenge and one that many adults couldn't manage. But by eighteen Mom was more prepared than most people will ever be for marriage and motherhood.

At this point, Uncle Roy arranged all the marriages in the group. He had had a revelation in 1957 that this was the way it should be done. Prior to that, couples had carried on relatively ordinary courtships, with chaste forms of dating. First wives often helped choose later wives for their husbands.

But this method had begun causing problems as multiple men would say that they had had "revelations" that they should marry the same woman—and young women always wanted to marry the younger men, not the church elders who were deemed "worthy" of multiple wives. Alternately, some men would barter daughters for business favors. Having the prophet decide simplified matters.

So the church my parents grew up in was very different from the one my grandfather and uncle would eventually head. Uncle Roy believed that living as an example—not mandating strict rules—was the best way to perfect the people in their quest to become godlike. He was much more of a "people person" than my grandfather. Trained as an accountant, Grandfather tended to have different concerns.

Uncle Roy was already in his sixties when my mom came to see him. Though he was nearly bald, with only a wispy ring of white hair, his skin was relatively unlined and his riveting eyes retained a youthful spark throughout his life. His energy and devotion to the church were also unflagging. He sat in an old office chair with wheels, and would spin around when he greeted people.

Uncle Roy had a much more relaxed leadership style than our later prophets. He seems to have been beloved by nearly everyone in the FLDS, especially Mom. There was little doubt in that generation that he was a holy man. They felt he deeply cared about people and arranged marriages with concern and with input from couples. His revelations were more advice than absolute commands.

When a young woman felt she was ready to wed, she would present herself to him for consideration. A man couldn't do this. Although he might hint with increased tithes and displays of piety that he was ready for a new wife—and this could be quite effective under some prophets—he couldn't ask directly. Only women could.

And so, after welcoming her into his office, Uncle Roy asked gently if Mom had received a revelation about her future husband. When she said she had not, he told her to pray about it and come back. She was impressed by how kind and comforting Uncle Roy was with her—and how he seemed to be filled with the spirit of God.

Although she had never met my father, Mom had seen him in church and at "fireside gatherings." At these meetings—open only to young singles over fifteen—church leaders would teach about marriage in Mormon theology. Then they'd give the young people time to socialize together over snacks.

These socials, too, fell by the wayside under more controlling later prophets. Even under Uncle Roy, boys and girls wouldn't mingle more than saying "hi" to each other. But the gatherings were an opportunity to get some sense of each other, at least in terms of manner and looks.

Following her audience with the prophet, Susan prayed fervently. She asked God, "Am I worthy to have an impression of where you would have me go? Can you impress upon my mind what is right?"

And over time, she found that her prayers were answered with the image of the man who would become my father. As she prayed, the 6' 10" well-built giant of a man with dark brown hair and twinkly brown eyes kept appearing to her.

She wasn't driven by a sense of desire or attraction to him, she told me, just a feeling that God wanted her to be his wife. She knew that he was a year younger than she was, which felt strange because at that age it seems like a big difference. Still, his was the repeated image that she saw. She kept these thoughts to herself, however, not telling a soul, not even her sisters and mom.

And when she was twenty-one in 1971, fearing she would become an old maid, she went back to the prophet. This time, she said she had indeed had an impression about her husband-to-be. "Do you want me to tell you who it is?" she asked him. Uncle Roy agreed.

Softly, Mom said, "Ward Jeffs."

My mother recalls the next few moments vividly. Uncle Roy had piercing, almost black eyes and he looked directly at her. "You know, I've been thinking the same thing for some time now," he said.

"Oh my goodness," Mom replied, embarrassed, excited, and nervous all at once. When she got home, her mother said she had had the same vision! But Dad, at the time, was serving in Vietnam, so the wedding would have to wait for his return.

My father isn't sure how many brothers he has. He knows that he's his father's fourth son and eighth or ninth child. He knows his father has around six dozen kids. However, because Grandfather kept taking younger wives and having more children—even some who are the same age as me and my brothers—Dad had a hard time keeping track. He thinks he has at least twenty brothers—and he thinks his father had many more daughters than sons. At least that was true among the kids Dad grew up with. But he does know for sure that he was the only one who was drafted to serve in Vietnam.

It was his age and a low draft number—158—that got him. His only other brother eligible for conscription during the waning years of the war lucked out with a high number. The others were spared by the American withdrawal.

Like my mom, Dad grew up in polygamy, with his father's wives living in separate houses. During Dad's childhood, Rulon had seven wives—so my dad saw his father only once a week for dinner. Even on those nights, he wasn't a very involved father. Dad remembers him coming home so late most times that the kids had already eaten dinner and were off watching TV or doing homework. Uncle Roy didn't restrict media exposure: he trusted families to protect themselves against immorality.

Grandfather's accountancy practice was very busy and successful, which was what kept him so late. He also founded and served on the boards of several multimillion-dollar companies (most infamously HydraPak, the company that made the O-ring that failed and blew up the space shuttle in 1986).

My grandmother, LaRue, would eat with her husband, who would then read the newspaper or study scripture. She was Rulon's second wife—ranking high in the hierarchy of Grandfather's women because she was the one he married legally. But she was not the "Queen Bee" or favorite—that position was held by Warren's mother, Merilyn. This fact would figure largely in our later lives.

As Dad tells it, Rulon was not the kind of father who changed diapers or rolled around on the floor with the kids. In fact, he would only occasionally discipline his children; usually that too was left to the moms.

But every Sunday, all the wives and children would gather at Mother LaRue's farmhouse, which was situated on about five acres of land. The boys would play football, basketball, or tetherball and sometimes even Rulon would join in. Dad recalls growing up on the farm fondly, though he will admit when pressed that there were lots of chores that he didn't always want to do.

Dad reported for military duty on March 19, 1971. Although he'd gone to public school, he had kept to himself there, mainly sticking with kids from the church. In basic training in California, he had his first real experience of interacting with people outside the church—including African Americans. The FLDS—following the lead of the early Mormon church—preaches that dark-skinned people carry the mark of Cain and are satanic as a result.

This ugly racism was conveyed through countless sermons by

church leaders, in school and in church literature. My father, while not wholly buying it, was consequently not comfortable around people of other races, to say the least. He knew little about them and had had virtually no exposure to other cultures and peoples.

By August, he was in Vietnam with men from all over America, facing fire. The time he spent in the infantry marked him profoundly. As he puts it, "I grew up in a cloistered society in religion, but in the military, I was exposed to anything and everything that the real world could offer. I discovered that there's good people out there, there's people I don't want to hang out with—there's every manner of people. I had to learn that regardless of race, even as I was covering another soldier's back in combat, he was covering my back."

He describes his army experience this way: "You had enemy on the hillsides, and in your mind they were going to take you down with a rifle any second. You had the enemy ground mines, implanted in the ground, string mines. Your enemy was leeches in the swamps and malaria, so you had to take pills. Your enemy was the typhoon that beheaded one of your buddies with the tin roof that comes flying off a building and one of my buddies dropped dead there in front of me.

"And the next day another buddy goes down to a red coral snake bite. And you take over his mortar barrel and you go on. And on another mission, your lieutenant, who is dedicated all to hell to take care of his guys, is blown apart and dies in your arms. You're looking at panic, there's nothing worse. To have a comrade in your arms breathing his last breath and going from conscious with panic to God. Gray. Blank. You help his eyes close. And that is horrifying."

His voice fills with emotion, his eyes with tears as he tells me the rest of the story. "And there it is, in 1972, the Vietnam War had dragged on for eleven years and you're going, 'My God, this man did not have to give his life; this war could have ended five years before. He didn't have to die in my arms.' And so I learned what life is like in combat and I found out how fragile life is."

Dad brought those lessons home with him and he says that they helped him to make the right decision when, years later, he had to choose between his family and his church. Unfortunately, he also brought home another legacy: post-traumatic stress disorder (PTSD), which would affect his interactions with his family for many years.

But unlike FLDS members whose only experience of outsiders was limited to brief transactions, my father knew that out in the world there were many decent, honorable people.

When his tour of duty was up, Dad had no idea what was going on back home. The other soldiers must have thought he was some kind of celebrity, given the swarming entourage of people who greeted him at the airport. His father, a dozen of his wives, and numerous brothers and sisters were all at the gate, waiting to greet the young man they now saw as a hero. Warren was almost certainly among them.

Unlike many who served, Dad wasn't neglected or ignored by family and friends because of the divisive politics of the war. He was vibrantly welcomed. But he knew something more than a homecoming celebration was planned when he was told to ride along with his mother and father in their Lincoln Continental—rather than with the rest of his siblings.

"I guess you're wondering why you're here with me and your mother, and not in the big van," Rulon said.

"Yeah, that thought had occurred to me," my dad quipped.

"Well, the Lord has a wife appointed for you and I've been asked to orchestrate your wedding when you're ready," my grandfather told him.

And as he tells it, my father thought, "Huh? I'm just getting home from Vietnam and somebody's going to throw a wedding at me? I'm just getting used to seeing round-eyed girls again."

It was quiet for a moment, and my grandfather said, in a soft voice, "I suppose you're wondering who." Then Rulon asked if Dad knew who a certain church elder was. And my father did. In church, boys aren't supposed to check out girls, but of course everyone does. He knew the family by sight.

"It's his oldest daughter, Susan. She's quite a gem." My father remembers his father's exact words. And Dad inwardly sighed in relief, thinking "Yes!!!!" because he remembered that all the daughters in the family were beautiful. As my father tells it, both men and women dreaded being assigned someone fat or ugly because of the prohibition against rejecting a "blessing."

During my dad's last eight months in combat, my mom's mother sewed her wedding clothes. Her outfit was very simple: a white A-line skirt, a lavender blouse, and a white scoop-neck vest with gold buttons down the center. Her hair was rolled into a bun with the traditional FLDS wave in the front, though it was not as large and pronounced as it is now. This is achieved with bobby pins and a product called WaveSet. Mom would later learn to use flaxseed oil—a special Jeffs family recipe—for this purpose. There was no problem with fitting a veil: in the FLDS, brides do not wear veils.

The only members of Mom's family who attended were her mother and father. A larger contingent from Dad's family was there. The ceremony was conducted in the meeting hall of the building that later became Alta Academy. At that time, Grandfather Rulon lived there with some nineteen wives and dozens of children.

Grandfather performed the ceremony, sealing my mother and father's union "for time and eternity." My father had been home from the war for a week. When they drank champagne to celebrate, it was the first time he'd ever tasted it. The FLDS has a much more relaxed attitude toward intoxicants than the mainstream church: it views the "Words of Wisdom" Mormons take as a blanket prohibition on alcohol, caffeine, and other intoxicants as more of a suggestion. Early in Mormon history, Joseph Smith had embraced alcohol, even running a bar at the hotel he owned, so there is a possible fundamentalist theological argument for this stance.

On their wedding night, however, my parents shared nothing more than a bed. My mother had had no sex education, let alone experience, and my father took things very slowly. He was a virgin himself. During the war, he'd had ample opportunity to drink, take drugs, and womanize. But the only thing he'd ever tried was one beer—and that was because he felt obliged to a buddy.

Like my mom, he felt strongly about his religious ideals and values—and, in the army, he had also come to cherish the values of an honorable warrior. He told my mom stories and courted her and charmed her. Dad laughs when telling how he'd sometimes been called a "silver-tongued devil" for his ability to persuade people to do what he wanted—but in this case, his cause was righteous.

Over the next few weeks, my parents fell in love. Dad had to finish out his tour at an army base in Colorado Springs, Colorado. And it was in their five months there that they really got to know each other. That was one of the few times that they were both away from their families, living in military housing like any other young couple. Within two months, my mom was pregnant with my oldest brother, Clayne. Growing up with two moms who had had dozens of pregnancies, she knew the signs well and did not need a test to confirm it. She and Dad began making a life together, having a child each year between 1973 and 1976.

THREE

The Plurality of Wives

Dad's second and third marriages were also arranged by Uncle Roy. In 1978—five years before I was born—my father was summoned to the prophet's office. Devout and in good standing, Dad was not at all apprehensive about being called in to see him. He didn't know how much his life was about to change.

When he got settled, Uncle Roy asked my dad if he was "totally committed" to the church. He said that he was. He asked if Dad felt that he truly loved his wife. My father confirmed this, too. By now, Dad was getting very curious about what was going on.

The prophet inquired once again about whether Dad genuinely and without reservation saw himself living in the FLDS forever. Dad reasserted his commitment, a tiny bit impatient now.

"Then, if that's the case, there's a young gal who I feel is right for you in the plurality of wives," Uncle Roy said. "Do you feel ready?"

Not one to shrink from a challenge or turn down a family blessing, my father said, "Yes, if you think I'm ready."

Then Uncle Roy told him that the woman in question was one of Mom's sisters. Felicia was about to turn twenty-one: she was much younger than Mom. She was vivacious, seductive, and beautiful, a brunette with full lips like her sister. But while Susan's face is round, her sister's is more angular, almost feline. Dad knew her from visits to his in-laws.

In retrospect, he believes Felicia had developed feelings for him during these visits. Other family members sensed that she was flirting with him, but Dad had kept an appropriate distance and no one thought he had done anything untoward. At the time, he saw her as just one of a flock of sisters-in-law.

From what I could see growing up, Dad's second wife was never as devoted to the FLDS as her sister. In fact, when my family was later excommunicated, Mom cried while Felicia cheered. When she was in her early twenties, however, Felicia apparently saw Dad as a tall, handsome man whom she wanted to wed. Like Mom, she presented herself for marriage and told the prophet that Dad had appeared to her when she prayed for a vision of her husband-to-be. Uncle Roy placed her with us.

Proponents of polygamy often argue that when two women want the same man, if he can marry both of them this will prevent divorce as a consequence of adultery. They claim that this is much better for any kids involved—as they will all have a father who is very much in their lives. Polygamy supporters say that, as a result, conflict and jealousy are actually reduced. They also claim that sisters are typically better suited to being sister-wives than unrelated women. Neither position gets any support whatsoever from what went on in my family.

When my dad married his second wife, my mother was nursing an infant, my brother David. He was five months old. My father's oldest son, Clayne, was five, Don was four, Sara was three, and Aaron was two. Since Mom's wedding, there had only been one year when she wasn't pregnant—and she already had four boys and a little girl under school age. Clayne alone was already a handful: he was fearless and Mom actually dressed him in red so she could spot him quickly and minimize trouble.

Mom was initially excited to learn that the family would enter into the principle. She believed in celestial marriage. She thought she was ready for it. But when she heard who the second wife would be, she

gulped a few times and prayed for strength. It was that thing about re-
jecting blessings: those who do so are damned, according to the church.
Mom felt she had to be obedient and keep sweet, even as she panicked.
During the few months leading up to the wedding, she was filled with
apprehension, despite her prayers. Even during childhood, Mom and
Felicia hadn't gotten along.

My family then lived in Uncle Allan's basement, next door to the
house where I would grow up. Dad's second wedding was held right
there, with my grandfather officiating, as he'd done for my father's first
marriage. Because of their illegality, polygamous weddings are low-key
events, with no party or reception. Other than her sister, only the bride's
blood mother and her father attended the wedding, which was quiet,
brief, and somber.

According to our tradition, during the ceremony Mom placed her
husband's hand into that of her sister, welcoming her as her sister-wife,
even saying "I do." I don't know how she did it.

After a short honeymoon with Dad, Felicia moved into one of the two
bedrooms our family occupied in Allan's basement. The children were
given a third room—all five of them, including baby David. To make
matters worse for my mom, the walls were thin and her bedroom was
adjacent to her sister's.

Dad would alternate nights between them. It's hard for Mom to even
talk about how badly that tore her up inside, and how she had to contain
her feelings, believing that this was God's will. Susan accepted that her
sister wanted children too and that she wanted a husband who loved
her. She wanted those things herself. It was only natural. But the pain
that this caused still echoes through our family today.

For my father, although he was excited to get a new wife—and attracted to this beautiful younger woman—the transition from monog-
amy to polygamy was not as pleasant as it might seem. He tried to be
respectful of Mom's feelings—spending their nights together reassuring
her how much he still loved her. Alternating nights between his marital
love of six years and the intensity of his new attraction to his second wife
took an emotional toll, however.

He almost couldn't avoid becoming somewhat insensitive just dealing with so many competing demands. Dad regrets not realizing then how much it hurt Mom. He was exhausted just answering her pleas, coping with jealousy, wiping away tears, all the while falling in love with her younger sister and trying to keep his own emotions in check.

The dynamic was complicated and difficult—and made even more so by the fact that no one was supposed to be having the feelings he or she had. It was supposed to be a blessing for all of them, not a trial. And everyone was supposed to keep sweet and not express any misgivings or even strong positive emotions, because that was the way to salvation.

There was another reason, too, that my father hadn't expected having a second wife to be as hard as it was. His own experience growing up in polygamy had been very different. Dad had foreseen a lot of responsibility. Obviously, running a large household would take a great deal of energy and work. But he hadn't realized how many conflicts and conflicting emotions there would be for the patriarch.

Crucially, until my father was eighteen, my grandfather's wives had lived in separate homes. This had made living the principle much less emotionally challenging. Each of the wives had her own space. She could run her home however she liked, without interference from other women with different tastes and styles. She could make her own choices about child-rearing and disciplinary practices.

Further, no woman risked hearing or catching glimpses of her husband's intimacy with his other wives. A plural wife didn't have to think much about what he was up to when he wasn't with her. There weren't so many reminders around. Everyone seems to agree that this was easier for all involved.

But in 1967 or 1968, Uncle Roy decided that we should no longer hide our polygamy, that we should be in the world. He had long preached that the holiest way to live polygamy was to gather all the wives and kids together—and live united under one roof. Living together wasn't practical if you were trying to keep a polygamous lifestyle secret. However, I guess with the rest of the sexual revolution going on at that time, Uncle Roy figured that there wasn't much risk that polygamists would be prosecuted. It wouldn't be risky to live openly in plural families. Church members began making preparations.

At around the same time, a woman who had left the FLDS returned after her wealthy husband died. She had inherited millions of dollars from him. She didn't want to grow old alone, outside the religious community she loved. She wanted to give her money to the church—and join a plural family.

Uncle Roy placed her with Rulon. They used the money to buy the land for the five-acre compound where I grew up in Sandy, an affluent suburb of Salt Lake. About one third of the FLDS people lived in and around Salt Lake City at that time.

Although Dad spent eight months in his late teens living on the compound in his father's home before starting his military service—and did experience some resulting clashes among his moms—the tension was mostly hidden. Facing combat meant he had a lot of other things on his mind. And on the surface, everyone seemed to get along. But behind closed doors, the women were quietly and sometimes not so quietly going crazy. Still, before his family moved into the huge new house, polygamy seemed much more harmonious.

So, when Dad's second wife joined our family, my father was blindsided by the difficulties of trying to manage his own relationships with such contrasting women and the constant problem of mediating the sisters' increasingly antagonistic relationship with each other. While Mom was quiet and accepting, her sister was bold and demanding. While Susan was devout, her sister liked to skirt the rules. Mom was calm and steady; her sister, stormy and high-strung. Typically preferring to stay in the background, Mom was pushed further and further back by her sister's desire for a star turn.

Sometimes it seemed like they were having a fertility contest: as soon as one would get pregnant, the other would report her own good news. In 1979, 1981, and 1983—the year I was born—each sister gave birth. Like the rest of their personalities, their mothering styles were a study in contrasts.

Mom was patient and nurturing, believing in explaining why a child had to do what he was told and in using time-outs and other nonphysical forms of discipline. Dad's second wife took more of a "spare the rod, spoil the child" approach and would react with sudden anger to childish behavior that got on her nerves. This conflict was responsible for the majority of the day-to-day disputes.

Then, in September 1983, when I was nine months old, my parents got a new summons to meet with Uncle Roy. Mom and Dad had been away on a short vacation. He would alternate taking trips with his wives, though Felicia somehow always seemed to get extra excursions.

This time around, however, Felicia was the one left at home. When she answered the phone and found out that my father had been selected to get another wife, she freaked out. My parents cut short their trip. Mom and Dad rushed home to meet with Uncle Roy. After the usual preliminaries, the prophet asked, "Are you ready to have a quorum?"

That's what they called having three wives, the minimum needed to attain the celestial realm of heaven. As the first wife, my mom was to be part of the decision, although in reality it wasn't much of one because—wait for it!—no one wanted to be the person who turned down a blessing.

In his office, Uncle Roy introduced them to a sixteen-year-old girl named Vera, who was sitting with her mother. The mom's husband had died years before and Uncle Roy had married her, helping support her family.

At that time, Vera was slender, with long curly red hair and brown eyes. She wore large round glasses. This was not considered an under-age marriage: in Utah she was of legal age to marry with the permission of her parents, which she had.

And, unlike many of the marriages of teenage girls that would occur under Warren, this union occurred at the girl's request. Vera did not get along with her mom, and she saw marriage as a way to leave home. Outside our community, a girl in her situation might have had other options, but in our world this seemed like the best way. Besides, she was eager to join the adult world in the church.

A few months before the marriage announcement, my father later realized, they had checked our family out. After church one snowy day, Vera, her mother, and a few of her sisters and brothers had knocked on our door, seeking help with a stalled car. It made no sense for them to come to us—both of my uncles' houses were nearer to the church parking lot.

But there they were. My father went to fix their car, while they watched my two moms bustle about, preparing for Sunday dinner and caring for us kids. I guess our family passed the test.

Dad's third wife turned out to be shy, naive, trusting, and vulnerable. She had a very idealized conception of plural marriage, and of what having adult responsibilities would be like. She didn't expect the rivalries and adjustments that were involved.

I have no idea why Vera had such rosy expectations because her own home life was apparently far from pleasant. But whatever her original reasons were for wanting to marry, she must have quickly realized that living with a strict mother might have been easier than being a third wife in a home with eleven kids under eleven. Still, her bed had been made.

Now my father had an even more complicated balancing act to manage. As with his other wives, he was not immediately intimate with his third. In fact, he saw utter terror in her eyes on their wedding night. Very gently, he held her hand, said "Welcome to our family," and went to sleep.

He was very cautious. It was over a year before Vera became pregnant with her first daughter, who was born the same year as Felicia's fourth child, Miriam, in 1985.

In contrast to my dad's approach, some polygamists such as Warren seem to get off on a virgin's fear of sex. They use this not only for their own sick, selfish pleasure but to dominate and control their wives. In the church, sex is supposed to be for reproduction, not pleasure: the acts that are officially permitted are only those that result in pregnancy. As a result, many men don't feel moved to satisfy their wives sexually.

Without pleasure, sex for these women is just another obligation and often a source of fear and shame. Using birth control is a sin—even if the women are tired out from previous pregnancies and the family can't afford to feed another child. FLDS men also tend to want to impregnate new, younger wives as quickly as possible, to bind them to the family. Before a young girl has children, it's a lot easier for her to run away or just go back home to her family.

Of course, my father wasn't without lust or desire for his new teenage wife, but he preferred to wait and build an emotional bond as a basis for the marriage, rather than "breaking her in." That was the phrase some men in the church used about what to do with a new young wife. There were also issues at the other end of reproductive life. Because sex was only for having babies, after menopause it was no longer permitted. Women feared this as they got older; they called it "being put out to pasture."

It still upsets me the way many FLDS men saw women as animals to be "used up" and "worn out" by childbearing and rearing. Another example was the fact that at age fourteen—when a boy typically receives the Aaronic priesthood and joins the lowest level of the church hierarchy—his opinion is seen as more valuable than that of any woman, even his mother. Only men can hold the priesthood and receive revelations from God. With regard to women, the world I grew up in has more in common with that of Osama bin Laden than with the beliefs of most twenty-first-century Americans.

PART TWO

DURING

FOUR

Division of Labor

"Father in Heaven, please bless this food and bless our family, thank you for all that You've done for us," Dad said, and the rest of the family followed in unison saying, "In the name of Jesus Christ, amen."

We were gathered around the gigantic hardwood door that my father had found on a construction site and fashioned into a stunning dinner table. It was in the large open-plan dining room/ kitchen area of our house in the compound. There was a folding table at the end, to make room for everyone. Dad sat at the head of the table, with Mom on one side and Felicia on the other. It was Felicia's turn to cook dinner. Vera sat next to her. Felicia was a top-notch cook and had made lasagna, which was my favorite meal. The wives alternated sitting next to Dad.

The kids didn't have assigned seats. We'd just squeeze in on a folding chair or put the little ones in high chairs wherever there was space. Any fighting over seats had to be settled before Dad got there.

And, although babies would sometimes cry and toddlers would occasionally try to get up and run around, once we started dinner, the meal was relatively quiet. Kids would ask for food to be passed and maybe kick each other under the table or surreptitiously throw food, but we all knew that Dad needed calm after his day at work. If he didn't get it, he'd occasionally slam his fist onto the table, rattling the glasses and silverware.

If we wanted to say anything after that, we'd whisper to each other or make faces, but otherwise we'd pretty much behave. You did not want to get Dad angry. If you wanted to eat dinner, you paid mind if he wanted silence.

That day, there was no major misbehavior. It was my fourth birthday, I think—one of the earliest I can remember. It would have been 1987, during Ronald Reagan's second term. When I was four, among my mom's kids Clayne was fourteen, Don was thirteen, Sara was twelve, Aaron was eleven, David was nine, Linda was eight, Brandon was six, and my newest full brother at the time, Adam, was just a year old. Felicia's Benjamin was eight, Nathan was six, Patricia was four, and Miriam was a toddler. Vera had two kids at this point: Amelia, who was two, and Kathy, who was an infant. Including myself, that's fifteen kids—the oldest of whom was fourteen—and Vera had only just left her teens herself.

When I think back on it now, having my own young child, the sheer complexity of the organizational tasks facing my family boggles the mind. My wife and I sometimes struggle to get one eighteen-month-old changed and into her high chair; having four kids who aren't even toilet trained and eleven preadolescents to feed and clothe and chase seems impossible.

On birthdays, the mom who was cooking would ask what kind of cake we wanted, though everyone pretty much always chose German chocolate. That was the universal favorite, with creamy chocolate frosting. It was another of Felicia's specialties. Birthday celebrations were another thing that the church later banned—along with Christmas—but this was long before the big crackdown started. Again, as I think back, I am astonished by all the work it must have taken: not just feeding all those kids, but making much of that food from scratch.

With so many birthdays, there was no way all the kids could buy presents for one another—the only pocket money we had was what we could earn doing odd jobs like mowing lawns in the neighborhood when we were old enough. But Mom and Dad would get us a present and one or two of the siblings closest in age would also give us something, so everyone would always get at least two presents.

That year, there was something I really, really wanted but didn't dare hope to get. When I'd been in a store with Mom, I'd seen a pair of blue and white Nike basketball shoes that I fell in love with. I don't know why. I don't think I could have seen any ads for them, and the other kids around me didn't have anything like them. Church families had so many kids that new clothes and shoes—let alone brand-name ones—were out of reach. But I wanted them with all the passion a kid that age gets for certain things. I asked Mom to buy them for my birthday, but she said, "We'll see; they're very expensive," which usually meant no.

When I unwrapped the box after dinner, however, there they were. I was so happy I swore I would never take them off—and unusually, none of my brothers tried to take them away or deface them. We ragged each other a lot, but we also knew how rare and precious it was to have something special in such a large family—and sometimes even respected that.

Daily dinners were a whole-family affair for most of my early childhood, not just on birthdays. The mom on cooking duty would have her children help her prepare the food. Usually it was something like spaghetti or homemade pizza, with a vegetable like broccoli or corn. If we were lucky, even on ordinary days, the moms would make desserts like chocolate truffles or strawberry shortcake. And we always had freshly made bread, which made the house smell wonderful. Among them, the moms baked at least five loaves of mixed wheat and white bread every other day, sometimes more.

In the winter, if the moms were pressed for time, we'd sometimes have warm chocolate Malta Meal—it's kind of like Cream of Wheat—with mint chocolate chip ice cream on top for dinner. Not surprisingly, this was a very popular choice with all of us kids. No one cared at all that it wasn't your traditional main course.

And so this was the world my newly four-year-old mind was trying to make sense of. It was 1987, President Reagan was dealing with the exposure of the Iran-Contra affair, and the stock market was headed for an October crash—but I knew nothing about any of those events. In my world, what mattered were the politics and fights for resources in my own home.

Vera was still having difficulty adjusting to life in our family. Felicia was trying to make Vera an ally or at least keep her from being a true rival for Dad's affections or from siding with Mom. Mom was enduring. And all four parents were coping with raising fourteen kids, with more on the way.

Our house was already quite crowded. It was located on Grandfather's five-acre compound. A high cement wall with large diamond shapes carved into its gray surface marked its border. Inside were six houses, including ours, Uncle Allan's (two wives, fifteen children), Uncle David's (two wives, thirty-one children), and Uncle Joseph's (just one wife and four kids). Warren would later take over Uncle Allan's house—he hadn't been old enough to be married and get a house when the compound was built.

Not far from our home was the building that would become Alta Academy. My father had helped build the immense white and pale yellow three-story building in 1970, but it was originally designed as a home for Rulon. Grandfather's former home had around forty-four bedrooms, twenty-four baths, and three kitchens. Downstairs, there was a tiled baptismal font, large enough for several men to stand in four to five feet of water.

One floor up was a meeting room that could hold hundreds of people. The prophet would hold services there for church members in Salt Lake and then fly in his Learjet to preach down in Short Creek, which is what we called the twin border towns of Colorado City, Arizona, and Hildale, Utah, where the other two-thirds of our people lived.

But the Alta building's most unusual feature was a network of hidden passageways and compartments. Those who knew about them could move between certain rooms undetected or hide in these small rooms until whoever they wanted to avoid was gone. Many were carpeted and had full wiring with lights. One seemed to provide a secret way to leave the meeting room through a passage behind a closet that led to a door to the outside.

Some say that these passages were built to aid flight or shelter wives and children in case of a government raid on polygamists. This wasn't just paranoia: one such raid had landed Grandfather in jail for several months in the 1940s. Living in Salt Lake, however, Rulon avoided being caught in what was until recently the country's biggest anti-polygamy raid—the 1953 raid on Short Creek, which had split hundreds of families for at least two years. Two-hundred sixty-three children were taken into custody back then. In 2008, of course, Texas would take some 439 children out of an FLDS compound in Eldorado.[1]

But when Dad helped build Grandfather's home, he told me, the secret hallways and hiding holes weren't there. He thinks they may have been added when it was converted into a school. I know from personal experience that they may then have been used for much more sinister purposes.

Next door to my school was the house Grandfather moved into after Alta Academy opened in 1973: an 8,300-square-foot, twenty-three-bedroom, ten-bath mansion. It too had numerous secret hideaways and escape corridors.

Our home was much smaller and less strange. It had three levels and eight bedrooms. The main floor was a big, open space, with a large kitchen and dining area and a big, formal living room. Up the stairs on the left side of the house was my mom's bedroom, which had a peaked roof.

My twin bed—which I would soon share with my younger brother Adam—was in a large hallway that led to my mom's room. Our dressers—which were almost sacred to us, as they were the only places that were ours alone—lined one wall. As a child, I kept my most prized possessions there, where no one else was allowed to touch them. This was a precious bit of personal space in a world where privacy was extremely rare.

On the other end of the house, accessible by a staircase, was my older brothers' bedroom. There were usually four or five of them there, in a room with twin bunk beds under the other peak of the roof. Felicia's bedroom was in the basement, on the opposite side of the house to where my mom lived.

On Mom's side of the basement was Vera's room, a small rec room, and a nook that we later used for a computer. Felicia's boys, Benjamin and Nathan, occupied a nearby bedroom. Sara and Linda also shared a bedroom down there, as did Patricia, Miriam, and Amelia. Kids were everywhere.

Not surprisingly, organization was critical to life in our growing family. Kids were assigned a rotation of chores to make sure everything got done. Loading the dishwasher, sweeping the floor, cleaning the porch—everything was spelled out. When he had had two wives, my dad decided that one should do kitchen duty each day, the other child care. When Vera joined the rotation, every wife had the third day off.

A big chart laid out the children's duties, which changed with age. And for all of us, there was no choice but to help out with child care—there were always infants and toddlers around. As each of us—boys and girls—grew, we were immediately drafted by the moms to use our new skills to help in whatever way we could. Even a three-year-old, for example, can help calm a baby or bring Mom a bottle or an item of clothing. A four-year-old can do more. As soon as we were physically capable of helping, we did.

In fact, when my brother Martin had colic and I was just eight, I was the one who got up at night to feed and soothe him because my mom had broken her back when she slipped on a toy and fell down the stairs. His crib was in my "room" in the hall. I tried everything I could think of to calm him down, but until he was a year old, he just screamed most of the night and much of the day, too. I'd try rocking him and giving him a bottle and bringing him in to Mom for comfort, but nothing worked for very long.

Though we didn't appreciate it at the time, with all this experience, there's not a man in my family who doesn't know how to change a diaper or feed and hold an infant. In fact, when I got married to Jody—who had never been in our church—I was much more relaxed with my newborn daughter than Jody was.

That said, I'm extremely grateful that my wife and I can afford disposable diapers. As a kid, I probably spent more time washing cloth diapers out in the toilet than many moms do. I was not at all happy about cleaning my younger siblings' diapers, but I didn't even think to protest. Sometimes, however, I would "accidentally" flush them down the toilet—if you did it right, it wouldn't clog. But mostly, I just saw it as part of what we all did. If we'd used disposables in my family, we probably wouldn't have been able to afford to eat.

Laundry was a constant chore. There was only one large washer and dryer and the moms were supposed to alternate days to use them to do their own clothes and those of their children. This was not the best arrangement for my mom: she had nearly twice as many kids as her sister did and Dad's third wife, Vera, had only two. Mom had to beg extra time on the machines from the other wives on their laundry days, which became a source of conflict.

As you might imagine, running such a large household was both complicated and expensive. On top of working and being in charge of the outdoor chores, Dad managed our finances because he did not want one wife to have the "power of the purse" over her sister-wives. Because he had so much else to do, sometimes bills would fall by the wayside. Then there would be late fees and everyone would have to scramble even more than usual.

At the peak of our family's earnings during my childhood, our household income was about $100,000, with my dad bringing in most of it. But often it was less, and with a minimum of ten people in the household and often more than double that, even in Salt Lake City, a hundred grand doesn't go very far. When I was little, my dad worked construction. At one point, he owned a home-remodeling firm called Crown Design. He later worked for an injection-molding company, owned by some of his brothers—ultimately becoming a vice president of marketing. That job took him around the world, so he would often be away from home on sales trips.

To help support us, my mom and her sister both worked several days a week as house cleaners, tidying up for the wealthy homeowners who lived in our neighborhood. Sometimes they'd bring a few of the younger kids to help out. Everyone worked. When I was in middle school, a bunch of us had to take jobs after school, on the assembly line at Uncle Dave's factory. He made NuSkin products. We would put soap into soap dishes, then wrap them in plastic. Most of us boys did construction work, too—starting at about age twelve or thirteen. Usually, everyone turned most or all of what we made over to our father.

Another resource for some of the family was food stamps. During my childhood, the prophet had begun preaching about "bleeding the beast." This meant using the government, which we believed was wicked and corrupt, to our advantage. We could weaken it while enriching ourselves, which was seen as a good thing. Mom wasn't eligible for food stamps because she was legally married. Felicia would have been much too proud to apply otherwise, but with the church's encouragement, she did. After all, she was officially a single mother—so technically, she appeared to meet the requirements.

Her bonus, however, soon became a bone of contention among the wives. She would use the extra money that she no longer had to spend on food to treat herself and her own kids, rather than turning it over to Dad. She argued that it was her money and it should not go into a household that she wasn't supposed to belong to to be eligible for it. She would even get extra dinner dates at restaurants with Dad because he would agree to go since he didn't have to take money out of our household account to pay for them. Not surprisingly, Mom and Vera were not happy about this.

Groceries alone cost hundreds of dollars a month. We didn't have to buy everything, fortunately. We grew most of our vegetables in a garden that was more like a small farm: about 100 by 150 feet long. We got milk from a neighboring family who had cows and gave their milk to the church, like a tithe. Mom and her sister-wives would get milk in a five-gallon bucket and sometimes they'd make some of it into fresh butter.

Because they baked so much bread anyway, the moms would sometimes share it with the neighbors. There was an informal economy of barter that helped sustain us. For example, one family that Mom worked for owned a meat company, so she'd sometimes trade her work for half a cow and we'd have beef for a few months. Some people had planted fruit trees, so we'd get fruit from them. For a time, we raised turkeys. Dad would slaughter them, saying "You ready kids?" and whack! He'd chop off the head in one stroke so as not to bruise the meat.

Most everything else had to come from the store. Once a week, whichever mom was on kitchen duty would take one or two kids with her to help haul the three or four carts she'd eventually fill at Smith's, a supermarket in a strip mall a few miles down the mountain. We'd all fight to go to the store because whoever went could often slip a few items he or she wanted into a cart, where they would go unnoticed amid dozens, even hundreds, of other items. All of the moms became masters at clipping coupons and spotting bargains. Frugality was a necessity.

Still, despite all of our contributions, things were always tight. Most of our clothing came from the Deseret Industries thrift shops, which were run by the main Mormon church. Even the moms had to get their clothes there. This embarrassed Felicia, who would sometimes tell people that a particular item had come from "Carol's Boutique" instead. It was worse for us kids, though: an item bought for an older child would be handed down from one sibling to another until it was completely unwearable or outgrown by everyone.

Even our underwear was bought secondhand. Fortunately, for my early childhood, we weren't required to wear the long underwear that Warren would mandate later. My moms made some of our family's clothing by hand as well, but they were mostly too busy with outside work and household duties.

Unsurprisingly, finances were a frequent source of friction. Money was both a limited resource and a potent symbol of attention and affection. On some level, everyone monitored every purchase made for any sign of unfairness or favoritism. Since we couldn't talk about what was really going on, these disputes became proxies for deeper issues. The battles were fierce. They weren't about money but about love.

FIVE

Extremes

"How dare you touch my kids!" my mother was screaming at Felicia, shouting at the top of her lungs over the din of toddlers screeching, babies crying, and boys messing with each other. It was 1988, I was five now. It was Mom's day to cook, so I was helping out in the kitchen, probably setting the table or something like that.

My full older siblings—Clayne, Don, Sara, Aaron, David, Linda, and Brandon—were all there, everyone assigned a role from chopping vegetables and stirring sauces to washing dishes. Vera was hiding in her room, as she tried to do whenever there was conflict.

Mom had seen the bruises I'd gotten after Felicia's daughter Patricia had told on me for "hitting" her. Just like her mom, Patricia seemed to be the apple of Dad's eye. She was a pretty little girl, with blond hair and big brown eyes, but she always had to have her way. As Mom continued to yell, she picked up Adam, who was bawling because Miriam had taken a toy away from him, stopping to calm him and put him back down.

Someone was trying to play the piano in the living room while one of the toddlers joined in, plinking random keys. Most of us had had a few years of lessons from a lady in the church who lived nearby, but no one practiced enough and no one seemed to have particular talent.

I hadn't actually hit Patricia. We'd been taught early on not to hit girls. But she had come home from the store with yet another princess doll while none of my mom's kids had gotten anything. I didn't want her stupid doll; I was just tired of her rubbing it in our faces that she could get whatever she wanted while we were told "No, we can't afford that." And I couldn't stand that smug grin she had when she showed off her doll, shrieking as I chased her around the house.

When I'd caught her and tried to grab it, she'd scratched my face, catching my cheek with a jagged nail and making me bleed. I held her arms back, not intending to hurt her, just wanting to keep her off me. But of course, she ran to her mother, who was on babysitting duty while my mom was at work. Patricia was in tears and then her mom yelled.

"What the hell do you think you're doing? You damn kids never let me have a moment's peace, you little shitheads."

If I had sworn like that, Felicia would have forced me to swallow a tablespoon of Tabasco sauce or cayenne pepper powder, without water, giving me a tremendously painful burn that often made me vomit. But she could say and do whatever she wanted, just like her little princess Patricia.

This time Felicia grabbed me so hard that it bruised my wrist, and then she started waling on my back with a belt. That had left raised red welts and purpled bruises, which I had shown my mother. Now Felicia had to deal with Mom.

"How dare you!" my mom said again to her sister. "I told you I do not want you touching my kids. Just leave it for me when I get home."

Felicia replied that if she did it Mom's way, everyone would run wild. The kids were out of control, they needed more discipline. Even though Mom wasn't hit when the sisters were growing up, Felicia had been because she was much more rebellious. So she thought physical punishment worked. But Mom pointed to the heavy bruises and welts on my back and thighs. "You can't do that," she said, shaking her head. "He's just a little kid. You really hurt him."

Felicia said that if I had behaved myself, it wouldn't have happened. "He's always such a little shit," she said. "He's always provoking her."

"Don't talk about my children that way," my mom screamed back. They were really close to each other now. One of them shoved the other, I don't know who. Then my mom grabbed her sister's hair and Felicia fought back. In seconds they were rolling on the floor, trying to scratch each other's faces. Seeing this, one of the littler kids started bawling and I tried to get out of the way. Soon several toddlers were crying. None of us knew what to do.

Just then, Dad arrived and pulled them apart, giving each a look that said he'd had a hard day at work and didn't want to deal with problems at home. "Stop," he said, and the edge in his voice was enough to make everyone mind.

In many marriages, child discipline rivals sex and money as a major source of conflict: the different backgrounds and personalities of most spouses make some disagreement all but inevitable. But when you've got four people in a marriage with fifteen kids, the issue is bound to be contentious—particularly when two are sisters who don't get along, the third is a sixteen-year-old girl who got married at least in part in an effort to flee a troubled family, and the man of the house suffers post-traumatic stress disorder resulting in unpredictable rage.

As a young child, though, I couldn't really understand the tensions and power struggles. I've been told that trauma can fracture your memory and that was certainly the case for me. Looking back, my childhood was like my home state of Utah—a picture of sharp contrasts, with potentially deadly extremes and a harsh climate, lifeless deserts offset by green valleys and interrupted by high peaks of breathtaking beauty.

At home I would flip from feeling lost in the crowd to feeling loved and safe in my family, from playing happily with my siblings to bitterly fighting with them for any scrap of attention or affection I could get from Mom and Dad. Later, after my nightmare began, fear alternated with numbness, disconnected from their original source. So the stories of my childhood are either idyllic, horrific, or filled with a sense of unreality.

But there was a certain logic to the struggles, which became clear to me much later. It had to do with how our family had been constructed—and with the difficulty Vera had coping with so many children.

Vera came into our family when I was less than a year old, and because my mom and Felicia were working part time then, she carried an extra burden of babysitting. There were eleven kids under eleven in our house—and Vera would be left home several days a week with all of them, none of whom were her blood children. This started when she had lived with us for only a month or two.

I realize now that she must have been completely overwhelmed. I can also understand as an adult that her behavior must have been driven to some extent by her troubled childhood. But all I knew as a kid was that she hated boys and she had nine to contend with. Nothing we did was ever okay with her; nothing pleased her. She had a hot temper to go with her bright red hair and just seemed mean and vindictive.

My parents tell me that when I was about a year old, Vera completely lost it one day and tried to smother me. She had been feeding me and I apparently didn't want to eat any more. I started crying and she shoved the food into my mouth, holding it closed. Clayne, who was about ten, saw that I was turning blue. He screamed. She held on.

He ran to the phone and called my mom, panic stricken. "Vera's trying to kill Brent," he said. Vera ran out of the room, leaving me in the high chair, bawling. Mom dropped everything and raced home. But Vera got in her car and took off before my mother got there. I guess she couldn't deal with what had happened. She slunk back home later that day, when things had cooled down, went to her room, and closed the door.

But even that incident didn't excuse her from child care. My parents really didn't have a choice: we needed the money the other moms made at work, and they couldn't afford day care. Sometimes, Vera would hit us with these large wooden Lincoln Logs toys, which were an inch and a half square and one to two feet long. They really hurt. Alternatively, she would beat us with wire hangers or metal cooking spoons.

She had three kids with my dad: Amelia, Kathy, and Nadine. Amelia was two years younger than me, with brown hair and eyes like my dad. She was very quiet—I think her mother's behavior scared her. But she was kind and all the moms loved her because she would do things like helping with the dishes without being asked or assigned. Obviously, that was rather unusual for a child!

Her sister Kathy, on the other hand, who was born a year after Amelia, was quiet but sneaky. She looked much like Amelia. But she would tattle on us for things we hadn't done and then stand there smirking or even laughing out loud while her mom hit us. We came to hate her almost as much as we hated her mom.

And so, while I had a close relationship with my mom and many of my brothers and sisters, the rivalry between my dad's three sister-wives and their frequent clashes shadowed much of my childhood. To make matters worse, although we didn't know what was wrong until years later, Dad's PTSD made his temper frightening.

His role as head of a family that grew to include twenty-five people kept him busy and hard to approach. Soon my uncle Warren would bring his own brand of darkness into my family—and to the whole FLDS through his vicious actions as he consolidated his power as my grandfather became increasingly frail and tired.

Nonetheless, the good parts seemed like a child's version of heaven. I had dozens of brothers and sisters and cousins to play with—in a huge yard surrounded by mountains, with lots of trees, hidden vistas, streams, fresh air, and places to explore. There was a large irrigation pond in the compound, which my grandfather sometimes let us use as a swimming pool, despite its rough cement sides that could tear your skin off if you weren't careful.

In the winter, we got an average of five hundred inches of snow. There was a whole side of an eleven-thousand-foot mountain behind a ski resort that was undeveloped. It was surrounded by white-capped, green mountains on three sides, and we took full advantage of our frosty playground.

Heavy snow almost always meant a good time. One storm alone could pile two feet of white stuff on the mountains. That meant a day off from school—and even without snow, few things are better than that. We'd sit at breakfast, eagerly waiting for the phone to ring and confirm it. Then we'd bundle up and rush outside. We had snowball fights. We built massive snowmen. We even borrowed all of the moms' bread pans to make bricks for igloos, cementing them together by spraying water from a bottle that would freeze each one into place.

Sleigh riding was our favorite. Because we couldn't afford sleds for everyone, we'd ride on the huge inner tubes of truck tires, first waxing them slick with ski wax. We'd all work together to carry them up the mountain. Then a few of us would climb on and speed down. We'd spend every daylight hour racing down the snowy slopes until we were so exhausted we couldn't even think about another run.

In the spring and summer, we'd ride bikes, also purchased second-hand. Boys being boys, there were frequent injuries. The main road to the ski resort was scarily steep, and we'd build bike jumps just off the left side of it. We'd ride as fast as possible down the mountain road and then turn sharply and soar. We'd catch ten feet of air and crash and burn in the dirt. We didn't even care if we got hurt, it was so much fun.

One time, long before I hit the ground, I knew I was in trouble. I was about eleven. Flying off the jump, I was going way too fast. I hit the dirt so hard that I shattered my right arm—the bone was poking out from my elbow. I raced home and said, "Ma, I think I broke it." She took one look and whisked me to the hospital.

Most other times, we got medical care from a nurse who was a church member. There was definitely pressure from our leaders to let God heal most injuries and illnesses and to use a church midwife for births rather than a doctor. When Alta Academy was Grandfather's home, there was a bedroom that was used for birthing. Most of Mom's kids were born there, but it was occupied when I was delivered so I was born in someone's bedroom.

I think our avoidance of outside medical care developed out of our desire to be a separate people, but I can't help but think that it also was a way to hide child abuse. My parents, however, would not shirk outside treatment if they felt that it was needed. It turned out that I had to wear a cast for three months.

———

We were crazy-ass kids and the moms were constantly worried about us, but even three moms couldn't possibly watch all of us every minute.

Our community was a strange mix of strict adherence to certain religious standards combined with lax approaches to many secular strictures, like safety procedures.

A good example of this attitude involved trampolines. Virtually every FLDS family has a trampoline in their front or backyard—and ours was no exception. It's a cheap way to provide wholesome entertainment for lots of kids at once. It is also one more way we diverged from the current American obsession with safety that makes many playgrounds pretty boring.

We loved that tramp—and found lots of different uses for it, some more dangerous than others. When you aren't allowed to watch TV except in your mom's bedroom under her supervision and you don't have video games or even many toys, you get creative in both positive and negative ways with whatever is around.

Just jumping on the tramp was fun at first, but then we had to add to that. So a few of us would lie underneath it and push up hard when the jumper landed, ideally adding a few feet to their bounce but sometimes throwing them right off.

After that, the tramp became a boxing ring. I idolized my seven older brothers—five full, two half—and always wanted to hang out with them. They, of course, wanted the littler boys out of their hair. So they were tough on us, brutal really. At first, if you did something that Clayne or Dave or Don didn't like, they would make you lie on your stomach with your face in the grass. If you didn't keep still, they would step on you or sit on your head and hold you there.

Then, one day, Brandon and I were arguing and the rest of my older brothers decided it would be amusing if they put us on the trampoline to resolve the dispute. Brandon is the full brother immediately older than me, by two years. We look somewhat alike, with dark brown hair and eyes.

Brandon didn't want to fight at first. He had this thing where if you tapped him on the shoulder, he had to tap you back, and he would get upset if he wasn't able to even the score. I think that made him want to avoid being touched. But they dragged us onto the tramp and I went for it, wanting to show that I could take it. The goal was not to knock each other off but to pin the loser to the trampoline, however you could. Kicking, punching, grabbing—anything went.

Because I was less hesitant, I kicked Brandon's ass at first. Since he was my older brother, they ranked on him for it. Our fights became a big source of amusement for the older boys until Brandon hit a growth spurt. Then I was done for. Now he's just back from his second tour in Iraq and I'll just say that no one should try to mess with him! Trampoline fights were huge with us for a few years until we got bored and moved on to something else.

During Utah's hot summers, our parents would sometimes let us sleep outside on the tramp. It was high enough up that we weren't afraid that animals that lived on the mountain—like rattlesnakes, goats, and skunks—would disturb us. We liked sleeping under the stars as the night cooled the mountain air.

Even Dad would come out from time to time, and we'd have half a dozen kids lying there, being calm and peaceful for a change. One night, we heard a loud ripping sound and everyone crashed through to the ground. We couldn't stop laughing, but we were also glad when Dad replaced the torn fabric the next day.

———

The highlights of my childhood were the fishing trips we'd take with my father. I was about seven when he finally said I was old enough to go along with him and my older brothers for the first time. We got up before dawn, at around 3 a.m. I'd spent days planning and packing my tackle box and rod. Everyone was excited as we filled our coolers and got ready to go.

It was one of the few times we really got a chance to hang out with Dad and have personal time with him. He was relaxed, too. I think he looked forward to some time away from his wives and all their conflicts. He drove us up to Strawberry Reservoir, a gigantic lake filled with cutthroat trout, rainbow trout, and kokanee salmon. We arrived just before sunrise, when the water was mirror still, with mist rising in sheer white wisps.

Dad had an old green tri-hull boat with enough seats around the sides for everyone. Clayne, Don, Aaron, David, Benjamin, Brandon, and Nathan—my dad's oldest boys were all there for our best trips.

Clayne had dirty blond hair and my mom's green eyes. He was outgoing, funny, and strikingly charismatic, a natural leader. Don—who is a year younger than Clayne—is more reserved, and very particular about the way he wants things done. He shares the slim-to-medium build, dark-haired, dark-eyed look that Brandon and I have.

Aaron, who's three years younger than Clayne, also has brown hair and eyes. He has a stockier build and an easier, lighter temperament, more like Clayne. Dave was a happy-go-lucky teddy bear of a guy, with strawberry blond hair and green eyes. He's in the center of most of our family pictures because everyone always wanted to be near him. He and Clayne were always laughing about something.

The next brother down, Benjamin, is just one year younger than Dave but very mild and mellow. He's got sandy brown hair and green eyes, but he's Felicia's, so he's a half brother, as is Nathan, who is two years younger than Benjamin. Nathan has lighter brown hair, with rust-colored eyes and a more sensitive temperament.

We came up with all kinds of crazy names for each other: Brandon somehow became "Damned On." Dave was just Big D. I got called "Wicket" for the Ewok character in the *Star Wars* series, though I have no idea why. Benjamin was "Gerber," probably because we wanted to call him a baby. As we scrambled out of the old blue Buick Park Avenue my father used to pull the boat, we would yell these at each other in the still, cold morning air.

Dad would launch the boat and then glide to a spot where he thought fish would bite. He taught me how to tie the bait to the hook. We used something called PowerBait, which is an artificial lure that comes in many shapes and sizes. We had a special trick, coating it with WD40 to hide our human smell.

With so many boys, there was lots of horseplay. My brothers told some crude jokes, but I was too young to understand them. What mattered wasn't what was said but just hanging out together, learning what it meant to be a man.

Soon Dad would say "All right, boys, settle down, you're going to scare the fish." So we'd sit back and hold our poles and freeze like crazy in the cold and damp. The biggest one I ever hooked was a trout that must have weighed about nineteen pounds. I was around ten, and that was one of the few trips Clayne took with us. He'd left the FLDS by then and I treasured spending time with my oldest brother.

Clayne was an avid fisherman. It was his absolute favorite thing to do. It took four hours to reel my fish in. We took turns holding the rod, till our arms got too sore to continue. No one could believe how powerful this fish was. Suddenly he surfaced, and we could see that he was a monster. But then, the line broke. Clayne was right on the edge of the boat and he jumped in to try to grab him, but he wasn't quick enough.

It was disappointing because it would have been a record catch for that lake, but we were proud that we'd managed to hold him for as long as we did. Besides, I think I would have thrown him back anyway. He was an old guy and had put up quite a fight. I was glad he could just live his life.

So there were good times growing up. I may have wanted more from my parents, but I knew that they loved me. Though my siblings sometimes drove me crazy, I knew they did, too.

A very young child thinks virtually any family situation is normal, since that's the only life he knows. Early on, however, I could tell when we went shopping or were otherwise exposed to people who were not in the church that there was something different about us. And it wasn't just that we had a much larger family than most people—we looked different, we dressed different, and we even seemed to carry ourselves differently. People would often point and stare, or even yell "plyg," which is a derogatory Utah term for polygamist. I could tell we stuck out.

At church and at home, I was taught from infancy not to speak to outsiders, who were "worldly" and who might corrupt us. This wasn't hard, since we didn't have much contact with them. I was told we were chosen, so while I felt different, I also felt special. If I felt as though I was missing out because of our way of life, I could tell myself that those other families weren't as close to God. They would not be saved. For a time, that seemed like fair compensation for our weird way of life.

In my early childhood, the church was nowhere near as strict as it became. We were allowed children's books—one of my favorites was *Winnie the Pooh*, which is why we named our cat Tigger. Later, Winnie and his friends were banned by Warren, who thought humanlike animals were sacrilegious. Ultimately the only books he allowed were the Bible, the Book of Mormon, and his own teachings.

As kids, we did have some exposure to television and a few select movies, but Warren ultimately outlawed these, too.

We were allowed to watch shows like *Nova* and *Nature*, however. We'd all go up to Mom's room to watch. There'd be ten kids sitting silently—a very unusual thing in our house—on or at the foot of her bed, hypnotized by the screen. I liked shows about lions and tigers the best because I am a cat person. When I was a little older, we'd sometimes sneak in and watch forbidden programs like *The Simpsons*. Oh, how we loved that show!

But when I was little, I didn't see or hear any media that exposed me to other ways of life. I just thought that we lived life as God meant us to, although some aspects of what we did and believed definitely made me wonder. However, I took strength from my family and it was this that sustained me as I had my first experience of the world outside.

In the fall of 1988, my parents decided to send Patricia to public kindergarten. Alta Academy didn't have a kindergarten, and I guess her mother wanted her to get a head start on her education. A few months later, Mom sat me down and told me that Dad had decided that I needed to go to kindergarten too, so Patricia wouldn't be on her own. I guess Patricia wasn't doing so well by herself. Whatever the reason, it turned out to be very important to me.

When I asked "What's kindergarten?," Mom told me that it was like school, but I'd be going with kids from the neighborhood, not from church.

I spent several months mingling with what we called "Gentiles," finger painting and singing my ABCs and eating graham crackers at snack time. The first few weeks were difficult. Patricia was still too frightened to talk to anyone, and so was I. I had to wear long shirts and pants, as was required by the church. All the other kids were dressed in ordinary T-shirts, jeans, dresses, skirts, and shorts. Felicia made sure that Princess Patricia's dresses weren't too different from what the other girls were wearing. Still, we both stood out.

Thankfully, our teacher helped. Although I can't recall her name, I will never forget her kindness. She pulled the two of us aside and said it was okay to be scared, that we should just know that she liked us and the other kids liked us and she was there if we needed her. She was understanding, not judgmental. There were other adults who were cold toward us, but not her.

She helped make sure that the other kids included us, and soon we made friends and even played with them after school. They were too young to understand how we were different, so they didn't taunt us the way older neighborhood kids would sometimes do.

Going to public kindergarten gave me something that most other kids in the FLDS didn't have: an implicit knowledge that outsiders weren't all that different or bad. In fact, some were, contrary to what we had been taught, kind and good. Like my father's experience in the army, it planted a seed and made me just that little bit less fearful when I would venture again into the outside world as a teenager. That early experience also gave me some hope as I later faced the great evil that lurked inside our church leadership.

SIX

Revelation Adapted to Circumstance

It's hard to imagine how something as boring as FLDS church services and meetings could have such a hold on thousands of people. You would expect that we had wildly charismatic preachers and testimonies and ecstatic music, which could engage and move people to tears and heights of joy. But my main memory of church is one of mind-numbing, soul-deadening, excruciating boredom.

I don't recall anything about Uncle Roy's preaching—he died in 1986, when I was just three. My grandfather took over as the prophet then and I spent hours in church being subjected to his sermons and, soon, Warren's. I never knew a world where a close relative was not our church's prophet.

Services were held in the big meeting room in Alta Academy. At one end was a low podium, on which the prophet would stand, flanked by his apostles. A large window, located behind the podium, bathed the prophet and the other church leaders in sunlight. This auditorium could hold at least three hundred people. It had bright, grass-green carpeting.

The pews consisted of folding chairs. An elaborate sound system, centered in a small control room off to the left, provided for amplification and recording.

Of course, just sitting still for hours listening to the world's most dynamic group of preachers would bore most small children silly. But what struck me as I got older was the constant, endless, seemingly mindless repetition. FLDS services consist mainly of preaching—not only do you hear from the prophet, but from the apostles and from other church leaders and male members who are called to share their testimony.

Hymns are sung at the beginning and the end, but mostly it's just men preaching monotonously. The hymns themselves aren't exactly rocking, either—Warren saw himself as a singer/songwriter, but from my perspective he didn't really qualify as either. His singing was amplified over that of the congregation, and it often sounded off-key.

"I am deeply moved, dear brothers and sisters, by the things that have been spoken here today, for the wonderful support and strength that has been voiced here in support of the servant of God,"[1] my grandfather preached in 1988, after hearing testimony from church members.

"There has been said here all of the things that I had in mind to say. I asked the Lord to cause it to be so. The key that stands out in my mind is that part which called upon the family to become one. How do we become one? By praying earnestly that we may have the Holy Spirit of God as our constant guide and companion. If all are imbued with that Holy Ghost in that family, they are one. There is no other way."[2]

Are you still awake? Grandfather went on, and actually this part is kind of interesting: "If there is a foreign spirit, a foul spirit abroad in the house, it must be cast out. And I call upon you all now, brethren, dedicate your homes. Cast out the devil and his imps and command them to stand rebuked from far off." He then went on to describe how he saw a large black "personage" at his office door one day. "That made such an impression on me that the devil is at our doors."

He continued, crusading against television for a while because it could bring "false and delusive spirits and the imps of the devil" into our houses. He read a long passage from LDS prophet Lorenzo Snow, the gist of which was that the Holy Spirit can unify our families.[3] Of course, we didn't get the gist; we got the whole lengthy, drawn-out story.

There really was only one message. We, your leaders, know the Word of God; you must obey us. Without question: Rulon even preached, "God said, 'Thou shalt not kill'; at another time, He said, 'Thou shalt utterly destroy.' This is the principle on which the government of heaven is conducted—by revelation adapted to the circumstances in which the children of the kingdom are placed. Whatever God requires is right, no matter what it is, although we may not see the reason thereof till long after the events transpire."[4]

So obey us, even if it feels wrong or seems wrong. The ends sometimes justify the means. We know what's good for you. We are God's prophets, seers, and revelators. Our revelations come straight from God Himself.

And that was endlessly reiterated by every prophet and testimony, in virtually every sermon and priesthood leadership lesson in school and at church. Grandfather Rulon preached, "Above all: Be obedient. Obedience is the first law of Heaven." And he said, "I love you and I want to save you in the Celestial Kingdom of God. So, if you will, keep the grand teaching that we are trying to get over: Keep the Holy Spirit of God! Keep sweet! It is a matter of life and death."

Warren's motto was "Perfect obedience produces perfect faith, which produces perfect people." You can see where this leads.

As a child, I would sit there and think, "This is so boring! I don't understand any of the shit you're going on about; I don't understand what the hell you're saying, 'Obey this, obey that, do all this'! What the hell are these people talking about?" I was so confused.

They were preaching out of the Book of Mormon. I remember wondering, "Why in the hell am I hearing this again?" I never understood, and I didn't want to ask my dad because I knew it would piss him off. So I never asked anybody. I felt like "God, I just heard this," again and again and again.

Later, I realized that that is part of how brainwashing works. You hear something so many times, it becomes a part of you, no matter whether or not you believe it's true. It's just there in your head, like breathing. You don't tell your body to breathe every time—it just breathes.

And so, the preaching wormed its way deep into my brain, with all its commandments to obey, obey, obey and fear hell and the "great and dreadful" Day of Judgment, which was, we were assured again and again, coming soon.

Warren's speaking voice also had a peculiar hypnotic quality. If you didn't know him like I did, it sounded calming, almost narcotic. It was hard to remember the specifics of what he actually said. He spoke relatively slowly, with long pauses.

He spoke quietly, in a low tone, so if you wanted to take in his actual words, you had to pay close attention. He kept a lulling kind of rhythm that was hard to avoid being entrained to, with an almost maternal quality, like he was trying to soothe a baby to sleep, like a relaxation tape. It kind of washed over you and crept round your defenses, speaking to the unconscious parts of your brain. It got to you, even when you didn't realize you were hearing what he was saying. And when I was a young child, he was already well on his way to seizing control of the church.

Warren's path to power began with the manner of his birth. He was the first son of Rulon's fourth wife. That doesn't sound like a particularly privileged position unless you know that his mother, Merilyn, was Rulon's undeniable Queen Bee. Though you might think the favorite wife position would go to the youngest or prettiest of the wives, that wasn't the case in Grandfather's family. Merilyn was neither.

She was tall and thin, with dirty blond hair down to her ankles when it wasn't braided or up in a bun. She didn't strike either Mom or Dad as a particularly attractive woman when she was young, but she carried herself with confidence and was adept at seeking and winning power. Dad attributes some of her strength to the fact that she was a member of the Steed family. The Steeds saw themselves as an elite in the church, with a bloodline that was blessed and destined for high rank. Merilyn brought an air of privilege to her dealings with Rulon and she brought her kids up to believe it, too.

Merilyn appeared humble, reverent, and dutiful, but slyly and stealthily she promoted her own children and interests. She made herself precious to Rulon and whispered in his ear in a way that made her whims and wishes seem like his own, my father says, and she had a way of presenting ideas to Rulon that made him think they were evidence of his divine inspiration.

Mom says that when she married Dad, she could see that Merilyn was treated differently from all of his father's other wives. Most of them seemed intimidated by her, afraid to go against her or even appear to have differences with her. Not having grown up in that family, Mom couldn't see why Merilyn had this power—but its evidence was everywhere. The other women would not complain about any of Merilyn's children's misbehavior; they knew that this would somehow be turned into a mark against them.

Dad personally experienced this phenomenon as a child. Once, Warren's brother Lyle ran over one of their sisters with a bicycle. The little girl was crying, and Dad could tell that what happened hadn't been her fault.

He and one of his brothers shouted that Lyle should have known better than to ride so fast where there were so many young kids playing. Next thing he knew, Dad was called into his father's office and lectured about the way he and his brother had spoken to Lyle and the "tone" they had used. Dad tried to explain, saying that any of the mothers would have yelled at Lyle for what he did, but Rulon wouldn't hear it. The lesson they learned was that for Merilyn's kids the rules were different.

Right from birth, Warren benefited from this preferential treatment. In fact, when Merilyn went into labor months early, Rulon was called in to pray for the health of his wife and her tiny son. It was December 3, 1955. There wasn't much even doctors could do. The premature Warren was so small he could fit into a man's hand—and so sickly, he was not expected to survive.

When he made it through those first perilous weeks, it was considered a miracle. This alone would have brought any child extra attention from his father, but combined with the fact that he was the first son of the favorite wife and with Merilyn's unbridled ambition for him, Warren was born to win favor.

In my father's view, Warren stood out only as a scrawny, delicate child, tending to fade into the background among his more boisterous sisters and brothers. He had no athletic talent, and soon came to prefer music, books, and art. He was socially awkward and shy. Tall and thin as a beanpole, as a young man he looked like the archetypal pencil-necked geek: dull brown hair, thick square glasses, a goofy, distracted face, and a clumsy gait.

But Warren learned his mother's tricks well. He was diligent and well behaved at school, graduating with honors in the top 3 percent of his class from Jordan High School, the public school in the Salt Lake suburb of Sandy. However, away from public view, it was a different story.

As a teenager, my dad watched as Warren began to mirror his mother's manipulative ways. He was four years younger than Dad, and much less popular among his siblings. To adults, he appeared pious and studious, righteous and obedient. He tried to be his father's golden boy, always seeking Rulon's attention for his good deeds while spotlighting the sins of others. He soon became known by the family as a tattletale and a scold.

In fact, he brought tales of others' misbehavior to his father so often that Rulon once banished him from the house, saying that he couldn't come home until he repented and confessed his own sins. The only impact this seemed to have was to make Warren more subtle in the ways he undermined others, hid his own perversions, and sucked up to Rulon.

It certainly didn't stop his devious—and deviant—behavior. As a teenager, Warren is believed to have raped a boy whose parents were not members of the church. My dad suspects that the child's parents were paid off. It's pretty hard to imagine that, but then it's hard to conceive of much of the abuse that Warren perpetrated. No one ever went to the police or child welfare authorities, even though what had happened was whispered about within Rulon's family at the time.

Dad believes Grandfather was told about the assault and quietly dealt with Warren, telling him he must never do it again. Merilyn's influence was also suspected in the lenient way the situation was handled.

One of Mom's half sisters lived near the apartment where Warren and his brother Leroy stayed when they were in their late teens. She told Mom that Warren was caught more than once peeping into girls' windows there when they undressed.

Mom and Dad themselves once caught Warren and a few of his brothers spying on them through the window shades when they briefly stayed in Grandfather's house, right after they got married. There was an outdoor spiral staircase from the first to the second floors near their bedroom, and if the shade was angled just right, you could see everything that went on in the bed through the window from there. One day Mom noticed the boys looking in from the staircase. She sat up and screamed—and made Dad ensure the shade was never left in that position again.

At the time, my parents didn't think much of it. But in retrospect, Mom sees a lot of Warren's behavior at that time as evidence that he was having difficulty controlling his sexual appetite. During this same period, she says, she became uncomfortable with the way Warren looked at her, especially when she was with my father. He seemed lustful, she says. He looked much younger than he actually was. And before marriage, he was forbidden to have any kind of sex.

Later, when Warren got his own first wife, he seemed to go out of his way to be physically affectionate with her in public, as though he was trying to show off.

After Warren graduated high school, Merilyn saw to it that both he and his brother Leroy were trained in their father's accounting practice. She positioned her sons to take over when Rulon retired. This gave Warren insight into the church's finances. Holding the purse strings offers great power in any institution, but this is especially true in an organization that wasn't always on the right side of the law, particularly with regards to accounting, labor, and tax practices.

But Warren soon decided to leave the accounting to Leroy. He had learned what he needed to know, and was more interested in controlling people than in counting money. Though he never went to college, in 1973 he became a teacher of math, science, and "priesthood history" at the religious school Rulon opened in the compound. My dad believes that Merilyn was behind the push to open Alta Academy—to give Warren a boost in the church. He soon moved up from teacher to principal.

No longer would FLDS children be subjected to the pernicious influence of public schooling. Alta would shield them from worldly temptation. Like the dress code that became stricter over time, a private school was another way to separate the church from the world. Warren could see that molding the minds of the next generation would give the church leadership even more control over the flock. Power—more than anything else—was what drove him.

I was about to find that out in one of the most brutal ways imaginable.

SEVEN

"God's Work"

For those of us blessed to be in the Jeffs family, there was an extra church session on Sundays with the prophet. He preached to the whole church only on alternate Sundays. Grandfather worshipped with our family alone on the other Sundays. Jeffs family church was held in the big meeting hall in the Alta Academy building. It was during those meetings in that building that Warren would commit some of his most destructive acts.

There were dozens of us Jeffs. If you counted just the wives and children of Dad, Uncle Allan, Uncle David, and Uncle Joseph, that would be eight wives and some seventy children. And that didn't include the rest of Dad's dozens of siblings, all of their wives, children, and other relatives, and his father's nineteen or so wives.

To me, the Jeffs church seemed like any other boring church function. Children under eight were taken downstairs to school classrooms so they wouldn't disrupt the services. The younger wives or sisters who were minding these kids would usually bring coloring books and crayons and other things to keep them quiet. At age eight, you would be baptized and then you had to go to regular church and Sunday school.

But there was a reason far worse than boredom that made me dread going to Jeffs family church. The first time it happened, I was around five years old. I was having fun with my cousins in one of the classrooms in the basement. The door opened slowly. Warren walked in and looked at the girl who was minding us. He quietly grabbed my hand and led me out of the room. He took me into a bathroom.

It was an ordinary bathroom that probably had once belonged to one of Rulon's later wives. When you came in, there was a sink and a vanity on the left and a door on the right. Through that door—in a kind of separate room—were the toilet and the bathtub. Two of Warren's brothers were there and one of them closed and locked the outer door. They stood by the vanity, as if they were standing guard.

The first time, Warren brought me over by the tub. He knelt down so he could see my face. He took on a very serious tone. He said that God had chosen him to help me become a man and that what was about to happen was God's will for me. This is how a boy becomes a man, he stressed. This is "God's work." His voice was calm, matter-of-fact, and patronizing—as if he was explaining a key point of doctrine to a kindergartner in the simplest possible way. But then, he got colder and sharper.

"You cannot tell anyone or say anything to anyone—because this is between you and God. If you do tell, you will burn in hell," he said, trying to make me feel the flames. He had this mean, vicious look in his eyes. It was like he was looking through me.

Then he told me to take off all of my clothes. I was confused and frightened, so I did what I was told. He put me in the tub and made me bend over. He put his hand over my mouth so that no one could hear me scream. And then I was in so much pain, there was nothing else. I thought I was going to die. Mercifully, I left my body.

I was never the same after that. At some point, everything went away—my feelings, but also all sensitivity, any sense that the world was a good place. I just went numb. When he was done, I put my clothes back on. I had no idea what had just happened. I didn't know there was such a thing as rape—or that it could happen to a boy. In kindergarten, I didn't even know where babies came from.

As he was taking me out of the bathroom, Warren looked at his brothers. His eyes were full of fury and hatred. He seemed to want to show off his power, like he could do anything to anyone and get away with it. What had happened to me was a warning and a message somehow, I felt. Both his brothers looked down and away.

Then Warren walked me back to the classroom, where I quickly scurried to the farthest, most isolated corner I could find. Immediately, I was in tremendous pain again, bleeding and unable to talk. I tried to curl up into myself and rock and hide. I didn't want anyone to see me or say anything to me.

I felt like I must have been a bad person for this to have happened to me, like it was some kind of punishment. I'd been told that it was what God wanted, so I must have done something terrible. Why would God do that to a good boy? I felt like it was all my fault, that I should have done something to stop it. I felt filthy and disgusting and repulsive.

And my feelings of shame were confirmed when no one even noticed there was anything wrong with me. I just went home after class and changed my clothes. In the chaos of my household, the squeaky wheels got the oil. If you weren't complaining or causing trouble, you weren't very visible. Dogs that didn't bark—or children who withdrew into themselves—didn't get attention. It was the only way such a large family could function. The physical evidence of Warren's crimes left in my soiled and bloodstained underwear simply disappeared into our massive laundry pile.

———

After that, at first, I lived on the constant edge of terror. I kept worrying that it would happen again. I was constantly on alert, nervous, jumpy. And when Warren did come for me again, I couldn't stop him. I didn't know how. I couldn't even explain it to myself, let alone tell an adult. He had so much power in the church that even if I had started kicking and screaming when he tried to take me out of the classroom, it probably wouldn't have made any difference. All I could do to protect myself was leave my body—but it seemed like every time I did that, I was less able to bring myself back.

I would space out more and more. I could never predict when the abuse was going to happen, though thinking back, it seemed like it was mostly Sunday mornings when I was in kindergarten and first grade. I know it stopped by the time I started second grade. I think it happened about ten times, but because of the nature of my memories, I can't be sure.

After the first time, I wanted to avoid everything and everyone associated with it. Since I couldn't really do that, I split apart. I learned how to suppress the feelings the abuse gave me and put every aspect of the experience in a box in my head that could never be opened. I just willed myself not to go there. Ever. It got to the point where I could even see Warren and not recall what he'd done.

I don't know how I managed this, but I felt that my survival required it. And it worked—for years. I didn't exactly forget what had happened; I just never remembered it in any conscious way. I had emotions and feelings and reactions that I now know were related to Warren's abuse, but I did not make these connections. I reacted but didn't let myself think about why. I quarantined that part of me off and kept the rest of me safe as well as I could.

Unfortunately, as a result, I learned to avoid feelings so well that I became unable to feel anything—good or bad. It was as though the world around me was a movie or a TV show, but I wasn't part of it and sometimes, I wasn't even watching. If anything even threatened to make me recall the abuse, I would leave my body again.

I would go into this state where I went through whatever motions I had to in order to prevent other people from bothering me and finding something wrong, but I wasn't really "there" with them. I didn't feel or remember anything when I was in that state. I just existed in a kind of suspended animation.

I can see that same behavior now in so many people who are still in the FLDS. Although they seem robotic and placid on the surface, you can sense that somewhere hidden in them is a seething tangle of pain and rage. Like me, they have been traumatized—whether by life in the church or by abuse or both.

And at home, I began to question everything I was asked to do. I felt like, how can life be like this? I was pissed off because I didn't have any answers about what had happened to me. I thought if I asked questions about everything else, I could get some answers and maybe not be so confused.

Whenever Mom would tell me to do something—clean my room, do a chore, whatever—I would ask, "Why?" And she would try to explain to me why it needed to be done, but I still didn't want to do it.

She would later say I was the hardest of her children to raise because I was always questioning, always protesting. None of her explanations were good enough for me. Any time I felt that any authority was trying to exert control over me, I couldn't stand it.

I had to take back some power. I guess getting a reason to do something made me feel like I had some. I didn't ask the "bigger" whys because I was so young, I couldn't even think that abstractly. And I was afraid to ask my dad.

EIGHT

Alta Academy

In 1989, I started first grade at Alta Academy. That meant that I had to spend more time around Warren. I dreaded it. Before that, pretty much the only time I'd see him was on Sundays during church. I think the abuse happened only on Sundays, but some of the memories I have could have been from school. Needless to say, I did not like being around him at any time, but since he was our principal, I knew that I'd have more contact with him once I had to go to first grade. And there was nothing I could do about that.

The school day started at seven. This meant that school day mornings were controlled chaos for us as the mom on child-care duty woke and tried to ensure that everyone who needed to be was dressed and out the door in time. Mom herself got up at 5:30 or 6:00, having learned from experience that if she didn't get dressed then, she'd never have time to during the day. If we didn't get up quickly enough, Mom would squirt water from a spray bottle in our faces, which usually did the trick.

Breakfast was typically some form of cereal, often hot Malta Meal. School lunches were made in an assembly line by us kids, with one portioning out potato chips or slicing apples, one doing sandwiches, and another putting it all together in a brown paper bag.

My first day, I remember walking down the sidewalk that led from our house to the school with my brothers and sisters and going into that big building, nervous and not knowing what to expect in class. It seemed like a very long walk, but it was really only a few hundred feet.

As it turned out, I felt more comfortable at Alta Academy—at least with the other kids—than I ever had in kindergarten. All the other kids were just like me in terms of religion and background, so I didn't stand out.

Sure, I had to wear dorky long-sleeved shirts with stiff collars and Rustlers or no-name jeans, but that wasn't nearly as bad when everyone else had to wear the same thing. Best of all, I didn't have to hide my background or feel like I was some kind of a freak, the way I'd sometimes felt in kindergarten and among outsiders in general. At Alta, everyone else had pretty much the same story.

I made a best friend quickly, a guy named Thomas. He was a tall, skinny kid with brown hair and blue eyes. I was pretty popular, but it was Thomas who understood when I had those moments where I had to hang back and tune out for a while. I would just tell him I felt sick and he let me be, without making me feel weird and without asking for any explanation. I felt safe with him.

But because of what had happened, I often couldn't accept being told what to do and I immediately started to rebel in class. I was a pretty consistent B student—it wasn't like I had any trouble with the material. I'm sure I could have gotten A's if I'd tried harder. I just didn't want to do things that made me feel controlled. I didn't want to be obnoxious or disrespectful to my teachers; I just couldn't stop questioning their assignments.

I needed to do things for my own reasons, and if the teacher couldn't give me one, I would freak out because I felt helpless. I now realize that orders or commands must have reminded me of the vulnerability I felt when I was being abused. Sometimes I would be so wrapped up in my own thoughts that I wouldn't hear what the teachers were telling me to do. Then it seemed like I was rebelling even when I wasn't.

And I never wanted to get in trouble because that would land me right where I didn't want to be—in Warren's office. Somehow, though, I couldn't help it.

The school day started with morning meeting, or "devotional," which involved about an hour of Warren's boring preaching. Everyone in the entire school had to go: first through twelfth grades, about 350 kids. The sermon was the same thing we'd heard in church: obedience, obedience, and more obedience. Sometimes, Warren would call on the older students to come up to the front and testify—which meant they had to say how great the church was and how they saw God working through it in their lives.

He'd always call on the brownnosers, the kids who sought favor with him. No one dared to say anything disrespectful anyway—but then again, even when I reached junior high, he never, ever called on me.

Still, I couldn't stand listening to him and neither could Thomas. We soon worked out that we could say we had to go to the bathroom and then sneak into the classrooms and hang out there, or even play in the school parking lot till morning meeting was over. Everyone else was in the meeting—there was no one to nail us. Eventually, however, the teachers did catch on. Thomas and I were both sent to Warren's office the first time we got caught.

Sitting outside in the hallway waiting to be called in, I felt dread in the pit of my stomach. I had no idea what would happen and just the thought of possibly being alone with Warren terrified me.

But when he took us inside, it actually wasn't too bad. Warren looked at us sternly and asked us why we had skipped devotional. "Don't you want to be a part of this church?" he demanded. Thomas and I looked at each other and I thought "Not really," but we didn't say anything. He preached at us for a while—that man loves to hear himself talk—but then he sent us back to our classroom.

As I got more used to seeing and dealing with Warren, I was better able to block out any conscious thought of what he'd done to me. If they threatened to return, I just spaced out. I could shift into that state instantly, and sometimes did when I saw him. I continued to rebel, but the connection between my spacing out or acting up and what had happened got lost as I pushed it further and further back in my mind.

Most of what we were taught at Alta Academy was standard elementary and junior high school fare. I learned to read and write, to do math—all of these basics were well taught. I didn't have trouble learning them. For some reason, the teachers were especially into cursive writing and calligraphy, so to this day I have really good handwriting. But beyond that foundation, our education in history and science was, well, peculiar.

"Science" was the most unusual, I discovered later. The teachers actually used scissors to cut the sections that were religiously objectionable out of the textbooks, and what was left didn't make much sense. Without context, it wasn't really science at all, just a set of disconnected facts. Instead of learning the fundamentals of biology or geology or physics, we were instructed on the church's accounts of natural phenomena. Evolution, of course, was out, as it is in many fundamentalist religions. But the FLDS's explanations for the evidence that supports evolution— like the discovery of dinosaur bones—were certainly unique.

For instance, Warren taught that God had made the earth from the scraps of other planets. Dinosaur bones were relics of this creation, not part of a prehistory that had occurred before humans evolved. Apparently, when you become the God of your own planet in the celestial kingdom, you don't get new materials to work with—but build your realm out of bits and pieces of failed worlds, like a patchwork quilt made of rags. Our God was given seven days to do it by his God, and here we are as the result, they told us.

We were also taught that man never landed on the moon, but I'm not sure why we were supposed to believe that. Asking why was a big no-no at Alta: you could get pulled out of class and taken to Warren's office just for doing that. Our religion was completely based on faith in authority. Asking for reasons was disobedient and ungodly and questioning was simply not accepted. I don't know why I didn't rebel by asking these bigger "whys," but I didn't.

I did think about them a lot, however. I would sit in class and wonder how it could be that there were millions of people and all kinds of religions but we were the only church in the whole world that knew the truth.

How can a God who created all of this be so hard on all the people that He's created, all the children? How could He put them on earth and give them freedom of choice to do whatever they wanted, but if they did the wrong thing according to our religion, known only to a few of these people, they have to go to hell? I always wondered, what the hell is that about? How can this little church be the only true one? Apparently, I wasn't the only one with these questions.

One day in sixth grade, a boy spoke up and asked how our people could be the only ones in the world who were right. I can still remember the teacher's reaction. It was as if she'd been hit in the face. She immediately grabbed the kid and dragged him into the hallway, shouting "You come with me. *Now!*" I don't know what happened to him, but we didn't see him until the end of the day and no one ever asked a question like that again.

NINE

Pulling Rank

When one of my brothers told me what was on Dad's list of chores for the boys that day, I groaned. It was a gorgeous summer day in 1991, the year of the First Gulf War, when the United States and a coalition of other countries had driven Iraq back after its takeover of Kuwait. Bill Clinton was taking on President George H. W. Bush in the race for the White House.

I was eight, growing up fast and trying to understand more of the power struggles that went on in my house, even as I felt crushed by some of them. According to my religion, I wasn't a child anymore. I had been baptized that year along with Brandon, in the baptismal font in the basement of Alta Academy.

It was kind of like a large hot tub, tiled, about five feet deep, filled with warm water. At eight, you were supposed to know right from wrong, so the baptism would wash away all your childhood sins, but any wrongdoing thereafter would count against you on your quest for heaven. We dressed in white, and as we held our noses, Dad dunked us completely under. We had to be totally immersed. Afterward, we went out for root-beer floats.

I was still shifting between blanking out and fury, between being able to enjoy the good parts of my life and being unable to connect to them. I was still angry and often confused.

To me, that day looked like a perfect one for riding bikes or playing down by the river. It was warm, but not too hot. Unfortunately, Dad had other plans for us. We couldn't play now: my brothers and I would have to dig ditches. Again! I was between second and third grade, barely old enough even to lift a pick and shovel, but Dad insisted that we all pitch in. I resented it and him. It didn't seem right that being disobedient when things were unfair would be a sin.

We'd had to do the same thing yesterday and my arms were already sore. Even thinking about lifting a garden tool was painful, let alone the thought of spending another whole day fighting the hard, rocky soil of the Wasatch mountains.

Worse, it was Felicia's day to take care of the kids, which meant there'd be no getting around it. When Mom was home, she'd sometimes give us a break, deciding that Dad had been giving us too much work for little kids. She thought that we should have more time to play. But Felicia wasn't like that. She liked knowing exactly where we were and would take Dad's side about chores.

Dad had taken to heart the idea that idle hands are the devil's workshop. He wanted his boys to know the meaning of hard work. He had also taken his military training very seriously and saw his service as an important part of what made him a man. His boys might be too young to serve in the gulf right now—but he'd make his own boot camp for us.

Combine his inclinations with the fact that we had a huge house, a massive garden that always needed weeding, and older brothers who liked to make the younger ones do their work—and, well, I spent a lot of time doing serious physical labor as a very young boy.

Every morning we'd get an endless list of chores. Dad seemed to believe that if he had to work all summer, we should too. I'd spend whole days of summer vacation pulling weeds from just one section of the lawn or garden. We grew most of our own vegetables and some fruits: tomatoes, carrots, corn, beans, squash, even watermelons. The garden was huge, and it had to be watered by hand, every single day. Now that we had to wear long-sleeved shirts and pants all the time—even when the temperature hit 105 degrees—yardwork became even more unpleasant.

But the worst was digging ditches, ostensibly for a sprinkler system that Dad said he planned to purchase but never did. The soil was almost all rock. These were the mountains from which they'd mined the granite to build the big Mormon temple in Salt Lake, after all. Our hands would get bloody, then callused, and our muscles so sore that any movement at all hurt.

We did start out trying our best. But seeing our cousins running and playing freely nearby in the compound made it very hard to keep at it. We tried. Soon, though, we'd start cutting corners whenever we could. Or we'd rush through the job. Sometimes, we'd just look at each other, drop our tools, and go join the other kids. We would pay for it later, but at that moment we just didn't care.

Some days, when Mom had to do child care, we'd ask her if we could leave some of the work for later and she'd just let us go. When Dad complained, she'd stand up for us and sometimes that worked. Often, though, we caught hell if we didn't finish everything to his satisfaction.

Since it was Felicia's day, we knew we'd have to get through the section he said he wanted done. There wasn't any choice. Brandon, Nathan, Dave, Benjamin, and I pounded our way through the dirt, cursing at the rocks and the heat. We were far enough away from her that she couldn't hear what we were saying and punish us for it. Putting it off wasn't going to make it go away, so we tore up the ground angrily. Afterward, we went inside. Surely we could go play now. We'd done our best; we figured we deserved a break.

But Felicia said no. There was some cleaning she hadn't finished. My brothers griped, but we didn't want to feel the business end of her belt, so we started dusting the living room or something like that. She was sitting on the couch, reading *Bon Appétit* or another cooking magazine. When we were cleaning downstairs where she couldn't hear us, we looked at each other.

"Why are we doing this?" Brandon said.

"I dunno."

"Let's go down by the river," said Dave. He was the oldest brother there, so we followed him. We all snuck out to Cottonwood River. In the spring, it was raging and too wild to go near, but in the summer it was lazy and there were a few places where it pooled into ponds. But because the water came straight down from the mountains, these were much too cold for swimming. Sometimes we'd dare each other to jump in and see who could withstand the freeze the longest. No one lasted more than a minute or so.

Other times we'd poke around with sticks or try to catch fish with our hands, never once succeeding because they were too small, slick, and fast. Even with fishing poles we never had luck there. We would also chase these small, gray lizards on the riverbanks—those you could catch, but sometimes their tails would fall off.

That day we were pretty exhausted, so we didn't do much, just hung around, glad to be away from the house. We made sure to be home before six, when Dad would get back from work. We didn't want him to know we'd been out playing.

But even though we made it back in time, Felicia turned us in. Before Dad even got all the way through the door, she was on him about how disobedient we were and how we'd failed to finish our chores. "They're just being little shitheads," Felicia yelled.

Dad didn't want to hear it. He had enough stress. He told us to go into the living room—now! He was yelling at the top of his lungs that we needed to mind our mothers. I nearly pissed myself—Dad was 6' 10", and even when he raised his voice only a little, it was terrifying. He never hit us; he didn't have to because his size alone was so intimidating.

Everyone knew better than to say anything when Dad was like that. We thought it was unfair, but trying to explain what had happened would only make things worse. He shouted at each of us boys in turn, then said we were all grounded. That meant we'd go to bed without dinner and had to stay in our rooms—away from the rest of the family—until the next morning. I was furious, but there was nothing I could do about it. Dad's word was law, and Felicia's star was rising, no matter what the rest of us thought of her.

Like the church, our family had a strict hierarchy and people seeking to advance in it. It was a patriarchy. In the same way that the church's followers tried to anticipate every nuance of the leadership's demands, the mood of the kids and wives often reflected Dad's. This in turn was affected by his experiences in Vietnam.

Dad's volatility and his status as head of the household—admired, almost worshipped—must surely also have played a role. The threat of "wait till Dad gets home" was thus particularly effective and powerful in my house.

Dad could admonish anyone, the wives had power over the kids, and the older kids dominated the younger ones. But the wives' rankings were somewhat unstable, depending on which one was getting the most attention from Dad. Most of the time, however, Felicia dominated, and as I got older, it became more and more clear to me that she was his favorite.

Dad didn't intend to favor one of his wives. He actually wanted to do just the opposite. He had seen what happened in his father's household when Warren's mother, Merilyn, became the Queen Bee. All of the other wives kowtowed to her and her children received special privileges. And Rulon's other wives fought subterranean turf battles to get the best for themselves and their own kids.

Dad had vowed never to let that happen in his household. But since he didn't realize how a wife can make herself a favorite, he didn't recognize what was happening until it was too late. While he spent a lot of time trying to be fair, he couldn't see that any failure—and there would always be some, since he was human—would obliterate his other efforts.

The personalities of the wives involved also made a huge difference. Felicia was more brash and dominant than my mom. She liked to dress flamboyantly and spent every other morning at the gym. Combined with Vera's youth and inexperience and Mom's desire to be obedient, this meant that, almost by default, Felicia got the upper hand most of the time.

Among the kids, we called the status maneuvering "pulling rank"— and even though I was a middle child, I often felt like a youngest because I had so many older brothers. They would pull rank to get the best seats in a car or in the ugly brown Econoline van that we had for a while.

They would pull rank to get the best places at the table or to make the younger ones do chores they didn't want to do. If persuasion didn't work, they used force. If I didn't do what they wanted during that day's ditch-digging, for example, I could expect to lie facedown on the grass with one of them smashing me into the ground if I tried to get up or even move.

Although there was the usual jostling for status among me and my full brothers, the real power struggle was between us and Felicia's kids (Vera's kids were too few and all girls, besides). Though we didn't make a linguistic distinction between "full brothers" and "half brothers" and "full sisters" and "half sisters" among ourselves, we all knew who their blood mom was.

Without ever being explicit, we came to see ourselves as foot soldiers in the moms' battles with each other for Dad's attention and affection. This was exacerbated by the fact that many of Mom's kids had a counterpart almost exactly the same age among Felicia's.

Clayne, Don, Sara, Aaron, and David were all born before my dad married his second wife in 1978, so they didn't fall into this pattern. But both Mom's daughter Linda and Felicia's son Benjamin were both born the next year, and my full brother Brandon and half brother Nathan were also age-mates, born two years later, in 1981.

My own counterpart was Felicia's daughter Patricia. We were both born in 1983. I was just four months older. While we often played well together, there were many times when I couldn't stand her privileged attitude and status.

Still, the maneuvering was plain hard on everyone. While I deeply felt the unfairness, winning favor didn't necessarily translate into happiness. Dad always looked like he had it the best, but the rest of us didn't have to deal with everyone fighting for a piece of us.

Felicia seemed as if she got most of Dad's time and attention, but she had to work really hard all the time to maintain her status. Vera sometimes nipped at her heels and Mom's quiet nurturing had a power all its own. Mom and Dad would sometimes get up at four in the morning just to have some quiet time together. I sometimes wished I had Dad's power, but I sure didn't want the responsibility that came with it.

TEN

Ammunition

The day of the big utensil fight, I was playing with my brothers at the bottom of the stairs, in the small rec room near Vera's room in the basement. Brandon and I were building cabins out of Lincoln Logs, not fighting, just playing—it was sometime when we were both in elementary school.

Then Amelia came by and she wanted the toys. She must've been three or four. We said we were using them and that she had to wait; we had gotten there first. She burst into tears and started throwing a tantrum.

Clayne was nearby, maybe watching some "approved" cartoons. He showed us what a big brother could be that day—and when I think back about him, I always remember the utensil fight.

At the time, Vera had been hiding in her bedroom, trying to have as little to do with us as she possibly could without drawing any attention to that fact. That day also marked a turning point for her in our family. Both Clayne and Vera would play a role in the aftermath of these events, unwittingly helping Warren in his plans to ensure that my father was no threat to his ambition to control the FLDS.

I don't know why Amelia's tantrum set Vera off. Like most of my brothers and sisters, I always dreaded the days that Vera had child care duty. Although Felicia would hit us, she wasn't nearly as brutal as Vera. I guess Vera thought we had been unfair to Amelia. Maybe she couldn't take her high-pitched shriek. In any case, she didn't think the problem was her child.

She stormed out of her bedroom, gunning for Brandon, screaming at him at full volume. For some reason, she especially seemed to target Clayne, Brandon, and me. I really don't know why. She chased after Brandon, hitting him on the head, arms, and back with a Lincoln Log, really nailing him. ·

Vera didn't discipline us in any normal sense of the word—she used us as an outlet for her anger and frustration. She would hit you with all of her strength, no matter how young you were. It wasn't at all related to the severity of the offense.

Clayne was in his teens then, and tired of watching her brutalize his little brothers. Vera was too scared to go after him at that point. He was too strong; if he fought back, he wasn't going to be the one who got hurt. That day, he couldn't take it anymore.

He grabbed her and snatched the Lincoln Log away, saying, "Stop it, he's just a little kid." She stood there stunned for a moment: no one had ever done that before. Usually, the other kids would flee and some of the little ones would stand around crying.

Clayne ran up the stairs, into the kitchen, pulling Brandon behind him.

"Get upstairs," he whispered to the rest of us as he went by, "and stay back." Nathan, Benjamin, and I dashed up to the kitchen, Vera following now, approaching the bottom of the stairs.

Clayne was near one of the silverware drawers, guarding the top of the staircase. He grabbed a handful of utensils from our ordinary table service. As soon as we passed him, he started throwing them down at her. And she's screaming, "Let me upstairs, I'm going to beat your asses."

By now, Brandon and I were behind Clayne, handing him more forks, knives, and spoons, like we were surgeon's assistants. As you can imagine, there were hundreds of utensils—two big drawers full—giving us lots of ammunition. I think Don and David came into the kitchen to join in the game.

And Clayne kept throwing. Vera continued shouting, but the clanging rain of silverware prevented her from making much headway. One of the smaller boys snuck down toward her to grab the utensils that had landed near the top steps, keeping Clayne well supplied. We rearmed him a few times, both from the drawer and the steps. After about ten minutes or so of this, Vera retreated back into her room.

We high-fived each other, rejoicing in a rare moment of mutual victory. Who knew what would happen after Dad got home, but at least for now we were safe.

———

It's stuff like that which makes a younger brother look up to an older one. When I was little, I was really in awe of Clayne. I remember him particularly at one Jeffs family outing, when we went to a big park in Salt Lake City. It must have been around the same time as that utensil fight. These were informal picnics, not church functions, held about once a year, in the fall when it wasn't too hot or cold.

Everyone would come—all the aunts, uncles, and cousins. We'd take over the whole park; I think Grandfather paid for it. He certainly arranged for everything, including a huge spread of picnic food and all kinds of games and activities for both kids and adults.

Warren would lead many of the games, but because it wasn't a religious event, he couldn't be his usual pompous self. There were too many of his older sisters and brothers around, and it was on playgrounds and sports fields that they'd always outperformed him. So he'd try to act silly, like a little kid. He just seemed ridiculous to me, and I think to many of the adults as well, even though no one would ever admit it.

Despite his presence, I loved these gatherings. You could play basketball or soccer and there were also games like potato sack races. They set up water balloon relays for the littler kids, where four children would have to run with a sheet filled with water balloons, trying not to drop and break them.

The adults would just sit there and watch us, laughing at how clumsy we were. We'd oh-so-seriously try not to break them—then fall down in a giggling, soaked heap. It was a pain that we had to wear long sleeves and pants and the girls had to wear their long dresses, but it was still fun.

Nearby was a river, with a really high rope swinging from a tree over it. At first, none of the kids dared to try it, but Clayne wasn't intimidated. I watched him, wishing I could be as brave as he was. I wanted to be as happy and self-confident as he looked when he climbed the tree and swung so fast and so far over the freezing water. He seemed so cool, so free. I never dreamed that he was living with the same fear and terror that so often paralyzed me.

But inside, Clayne was suffering just as I was. More than once, when he was in his teens and twenties, we would open the front door in the morning and there he would be, passed out on the cement steps from some kind of drug overdose. I was still only a little kid and didn't really know what was going on.

By the time Clayne was fifteen—when I was just five—he had been expelled from Alta Academy. Unlike me, he wasn't intimidated by Warren or the religion. Warren rapidly recognized that he couldn't control Clayne, so he got him out of his school as soon as possible. Clayne hadn't been a bad kid, but Warren targeted him, punishing him if he was even the tiniest bit out of line.

I would later get the same kind of negative attention in school, but Warren seemed more frightened of Clayne than he was of me. I was in the first grade ten years after Clayne had been that age. Maybe Clayne had been one of his first victims and Warren wasn't sure what would happen as the boys he abused got older. Maybe by the time he got to me, he was more confident about his ability to intimidate us into keeping quiet. I don't really know. But he seemed to molest boys only when they were about five and six, moving on to new victims when those children hit seven.

And so, when Clayne was in grade school, he was sent to Warren's office virtually every day. No matter what he did, he wound up in trouble. With that kind of scrutiny, Clayne must have felt he couldn't win. So he started fighting back.

As a young teen, he became brazen, heedless of consequences. He actually told Warren "fuck off" to his face! I don't know if that was what got him expelled, but Mom believes Warren was determined to get rid of him because he feared that Clayne could see through him. By scrutinizing his every move, Warren ensured that he could find or manufacture a reason for expulsion.

I don't really know when Clayne's drug use started, but it was very early in his life and it escalated rapidly after our parents enrolled him in public school. At that point, he really began to rebel. He simply refused to do anything: homework, classwork, whatever. He cut classes, played truant, drank, and took drugs. He'd take my father's Datsun truck out and race it up the mountains or go off with girls.

By sixteen, he'd been expelled from public school for selling drugs and fighting or actually acting as an enforcer when people didn't pay for their drugs. The dealing wasn't the low-level marijuana exchange many teens do, and the using wasn't the far more common experimentation.

He was hard core. He started using drugs like cocaine before most of his classmates had smoked pot or snuck a beer. He got wasted as often as he possibly could, taking the highest doses he could get his hands on. He mixed drugs with alcohol to get the maximum effect. He started staying out all night, and then he ran away for days at a time. He was a lost boy before he even left home.

Clayne was soon spending time in an intensive psychiatric ward at Charter Hospital. After two months they sent him to Provo Canyon School, which was supposed to be longer-term therapy. In reality, it was abuse. The people who ran the school had a clever way to prevent parents from realizing what kind of "treatment" they really offered.

They told Mom and Dad to expect lies about brutality, beatings, and maltreatment—but to disregard them as "manipulation" from an addicted child who would say anything to get out and get drugs. Consequently, my parents ignored Clayne's increasingly agonized letters begging them to take him home. They were doing what the professionals had said would help.

Mom and Dad had no idea they had sent him to a place that was the ongoing subject of lawsuits, detailing actual torture. They had rejected the idea that his problem was one of rebellion against authority. If they'd wanted tough love, they could have done what other families in the church did: send him to "reform." This meant sending him to live with a strict church family in Canada for nine months. They owned a logging company and used hard work and long hours as a way to break the spirits of disobedient boys. Failure to comply meant more work; if you wanted to go home, you had to yield to work and prayer. Or you could leave the church.

I would later see kids come back from Canada either broken or cowed, the spark gone from them—or so rebellious that they left the church at once. But my parents had believed Clayne was troubled, not bad: they didn't know what was wrong, but they thought it was a medical problem, not a moral one.

And they knew that this put them in the church's line of fire. Rulon and Warren viewed everything as a matter of morality and obedience. As school principal, Warren had already started to make it clear that he expected parents to strictly control their children's behavior. If teenagers balked, there shouldn't be any second chances. Disobedience was not to be tolerated; the forgiveness practiced earlier by Uncle Roy was a thing of the past. Parents needed to throw out the bad apple, stop the "rot," cut it off—before it spoiled the rest of the fruit. That was the way to be godly, not worldly.

But Mom and Dad saw Clayne as their precious oldest son—not something you could just "cut off" and forget about. Dad told me: "We were torn between 'How do we just follow the church,' which says 'Let your children go who won't follow,' and our love for this boy who needed family?"

After about a year in Provo Canyon, Clayne was released. But Felicia and Vera didn't want him back home. They threatened to go to the prophet. With all of the preaching about not tolerating defiant teens, Mom and Dad felt like they had no choice. Before he'd been sent away, Clayne had become close with a young man outside the church who lived in our neighborhood. His family graciously agreed to take him in while he finished high school.

And while Provo Canyon didn't end Clayne's addiction, it did seem to teach him to hide it better. Now he wasn't using just as a form of rebellion or disobedience—he was using for sheer escape. He wasn't going to let anyone try to "help" by taking the drugs away: that had made things worse. He eventually became a heroin addict, shooting up every day. He did not graduate high school and soon went to live on his own.

————

Back at home, Vera's behavior continued to wreak havoc. She just couldn't find her place in our family. By 1992—when I was nine—she'd had two children, Amelia and Kathy, born in 1985 and 1986. My Dad didn't want her to have any more until she had learned to treat all of us kids better. Although you weren't supposed to use birth control, he told her to take the pill, believing this was in everyone's best interest. He didn't want her to feel like he didn't love her and stop sleeping with her, but he didn't think she could handle more babies yet either.

This made Vera even more resentful. Having children is one of the few sources of power open to women in polygamy. The more kids you have, the more favorably you are seen by the church and, usually as a result, by your husband. Your children also tend to be your allies, so the more the merrier. Vera was already behind, with just two compared to Mom's ten and Felicia's four. She already felt like an outsider, being thrown in with two sister-wives who were also sisters. She saw being made to wait to have more kids both as punishment and as another way she was singled out for poor treatment. And that made her even angrier.

Vera was also the youngest wife in the house. Often youth is a source of sexual power because younger women tend to be more attractive to men. But it's a double-edged sword because the older women are more sophisticated and knowledgeable, particularly about strategies to get their way with men and in terms of practical information needed to deal with the outside world. Mom was more than fifteen years older than Vera, Felicia was close to ten years older. And those years made even more of a difference because Vera had come into our home as a teenager, while the other wives were legal adults.

So while Vera resented Dad's decision to delay further children with her, she also seemed to resent the children she had and the way they limited her freedom. Most of all, she resented the rest of us, particularly the boys. She was supposed to be a mom to more than half a dozen of us brothers, some not so much younger than she was.

Vera's anger wasn't limited to the harsh way she treated the children. At first, being a teenager, she didn't work outside the home. But she wasn't in school either. The days that she wasn't on child care or kitchen duty, she'd spend in her room or out somewhere with her kids. Then she got a job at an injection-molding company, doing piecework on parts of medical equipment. She was supposed to deposit most of her paycheck into the family account, but somehow that money never seemed to materialize.

Dad would ask her when she'd put the money in the bank, and he says she'd make up a date and claim to have lost the deposit slip. Then the other wives found some of the food money missing. This happened more than once. Sometimes she'd even hoard food in her room. Again, there were denials and vague, hard-to-believe stories.

Dad tried to overlook all of this, figuring that she was young and had a hard life. It was not easy fitting in with two sister-wives who had grown up together. It wasn't easy controlling so many boisterous kids. Vera would surely outgrow this misguided behavior. To help, Dad got her into therapy. It was only after that that she told Dad that she'd suffered some kind of abuse as a child.

In 1993, Vera gave birth to her third daughter, Nadine. She had apparently secretly stopped taking the pill. Dad was furious when he found out she was pregnant. He said that he had continued sleeping with her only because he believed they were using protection. He'd done that against his better judgment. The church frowned on it. He felt betrayed and deceived.

Around the same time, she'd asked to use his credit card to buy some school clothes for her kids. She kept "forgetting" to return it. It turned out that she had been spending her days off shopping, carefully hiding away the things she'd splurged on for herself. When the bill came, there was a $6,000 balance.

Now Dad was apoplectic. He stared at the statement in shock. He'd been feeling for a long time that Vera was not trustworthy. Now he lost all respect for her. He'd tried to do what he could to make things better for her. He got her psychological help. He'd tried to slow down the childbearing. He didn't abandon her sexually.

How could she do this to the family when money was so tight? How would he tell her sister-wives and face their complaints about having to pay the card off and scrimp even more when none of what she'd spent had gone to the family? There was barely enough money to keep everyone fed. The house was heavily mortgaged. Paying the bills was a real challenge each month. This was not how he expected living polygamy would be. And he had no idea what to do about it.

———

The Jeffs family outing in 1994 took place not long after the credit card fiasco. We piled into our cars: most of us got into the nasty brown van. The rest rode with one of the moms. But I noticed that I hadn't seen Vera or her kids get into any of the vehicles. Mom said that she'd decided to stay home. Someone wasn't feeling well, or something. That was strange but fine with me—the less I saw of that red-haired demon and especially her brat Kathy, the better. I jostled with my brothers for a seat and looked forward to a day in the sun.

I didn't sense any more tension than usual from the adults. We all seemed to have a great time at the picnic. But we couldn't swim in the river anymore. In 1992 or 1993, Grandfather had supposedly had a revelation that it was "worldly" to show off your body in shorts and T-shirts. That was what Gentiles did, and we were supposed to be more godlike than that.

So now, we had to wear long-sleeved shirts and long pants all the time. Some kids tried to swim like that, but it wasn't much fun. I didn't bother. I ran in some of the races and played basketball instead.

I noticed that Grandfather seemed to be fading away. He had an oxygen tank, and he seemed to just sit, looking very tired and confused. No one had said anything, but he must have started getting ill long before he had the major strokes that caused him to be hospitalized in the late 1990s.

When we got home from the outing, the house was unusually quiet. Vera and her kids weren't home, and one of our cars was missing. At first, my parents figured they'd just gone to run some errand, but she hadn't left a note. Then someone went downstairs and saw that all of their clothes had been taken from the closets. The kids' toys were also gone, as were the baby's diapers. There was no sign of Vera, Kathy, Amelia, or baby Nadine—anywhere.

A missing wife and children, an addicted son—things were not looking good for us as a united family in good standing in the church. We didn't know it then, but Warren seemed to be determined to find ways to marginalize any one of his brothers who might possibly be a threat to his overweening ambition. My dad was in his sights because he was very popular with his siblings, and these signs of conflict would give Warren ammunition. Soon we were all about to come under even more fire.

ELEVEN

A House Divided

The twins were trying to start something again. The blond-haired, blue-eyed angelic-looking identical brothers were actually little devils. For some reason, they had it in for me and my best friend Thomas. We were always fighting with them at school. This particular time, they'd appeared out of nowhere and shoved Thomas, saying, "We're going to kick your ass." I shoved one of them back, and then we were into it, punching each other, rolling on the asphalt of the parking lot we used as a playground. We were bigger than they were, but they were strong, so it was a pretty even match.

Within minutes, a crowd had gathered and a teacher came and pulled us apart. One twin had a bloody nose and the other had a few scrapes, but Thomas and I had similar injuries. Once again, however, we were the only ones who were sent to the principal's office. Warren called me in, and I sat down in my usual place in the chair in front of his desk.

He started pacing behind me, saying, "Why are you doing this? Why do you start all these fights? Why are you so mad?"

What was I supposed to say? By that time, I was in seventh grade. It was 1995 or early 1996. I'd been up there so many times I wasn't really scared anymore. Even when he hit me on the hands or the back with a ruler, it didn't hurt much. He was scrawny and had no upper body strength at all. I took much worse beatings at home from Vera. I still blanked out sometimes, but I didn't feel the terror that I'd had when I was younger. Maybe it was because I knew I was big enough to defend myself.

"They started it," I said. I refused to look at him.

"I don't believe you. I think you did it."

I didn't respond.

"You sure have been up here a lot over the years. Do you enjoy being up here? Do you like being around me?"

I had no idea what to say, so again I said nothing. I kept my eyes down. Then he put his hand on my shoulder.

I turned around and glared at him—and he pulled away as though he'd been burned.

"I'm going to tell your father," he said, and then dismissed me.

And when my father yelled at me later that night, I thought, "What the fuck? I see you fighting with my moms, I see them fighting with each other, what the hell's the difference? Why shouldn't I fight at school? I spend my whole life at home fighting—or watching someone else fight. The only way anyone gets anything around here is by fighting." I was really sick of it.

———

And apparently, everyone else was, too. Vera had left for good. We learned that she had gone to Rulon and said that she simply could not get along with her sister-wives—going as far as to claim that they were abusing her. Rulon called my father into his office. He was brusque.

"You are cut off from this wife," he said. "You are done with her. I am reassigning Vera and her children."

The church would support them and send them to Colorado City. Dad was no longer responsible, emotionally or financially. But this meant that he was to have no contact with Vera—or the three children they had together—at all, ever again. Reluctantly, he accepted that, still believing that his father was the prophet and that he knew the will of God. But his heart was broken over losing contact with his three little daughters.

Vera's departure also unmasked the depth of the conflict between Mom and Felicia. Without Vera to distract them from each other, their more subtle skirmishes devolved into open warfare. They couldn't stand each other now. Dad tried to mediate but had only gotten stuck in the middle. Everything became difficult: for example, rather than going back to cooking every other day, Felicia said since she had fewer kids, she should cook only every third day. Mom wound up picking up that slack.

Privately, both Mom and Felicia had expressed their dissatisfaction with the situation to my dad—many, many times. "I just want some peace, Ward," Susan remembers saying to him. "I just need a little peace." Felicia had now become adamant. She began insisting to Dad that she had to have her own home. She couldn't take this anymore. He had to do something, soon. It wasn't working.

Although earlier in church history, living polygamy in one home as a unified family was an option, by this time Rulon had made it a requirement. Dad was one of the prophet's sons. He lived in his compound. He was supposed to be an example to the community. Anything he did that was unorthodox would draw unwelcome attention, particularly after Vera's ignominious exit. There was no way that he could buy a second house.

One day, after finding the two sisters rolling on the floor and pulling each other's hair yet again, Dad made his decision. He gathered everyone together for the last time in the big living room.

"This isn't working well as one household," he told us. No one said anything, as that was very obviously true. I wondered for a moment if we were going to lose another mother. But which one? Then he said, "Your mothers want to separate the house so we can have more peace."

Among my blood siblings, there were quiet expressions of relief because we knew that would mean that we wouldn't have to be yelled at by Felicia anymore. That would be great for us. But her kids weren't so thrilled: they had enjoyed the days when Mom did child care and there weren't so many chores. Now Felicia would always be in charge of them.

Dad came home one night not long afterward with a bunch of building supplies and a plan. The first step would be a wall down the middle of the living room. It would have a door, but it locked from both sides. He put some of the older boys to work, measuring and putting together the framework. Next, he would make Felicia her own kitchen and dining area. One bedroom would become her new living room and a second laundry room would be built by the stairs. A side entrance would become Felicia's front door. Our house was going to be split almost exactly in half.

Now Mom and her kids stayed on one side of the house while Felicia and her children lived on the other. If we wanted to play with our half-siblings or do homework with them there, we had to ask Felicia's permission to come in—and they had to do the same with Mom. Dad alternated his dinners and nights between sides. Every third night he spent in a room in a guest house he'd constructed on our property. Before that, he hadn't had a bedroom that was his alone.

After the split, our side of the house was always busier. And this wasn't just because Mom had many more children. My half brothers and half sisters spent as much time as they could on our side. It was just a lot calmer.

As Dad continued the renovations, he applied for help from church members as a Saturday Work Day project. Saturday Work Days allowed church members to build or renovate their homes through the free, communal labor of our membership. If a man needed help with a home construction project, he could add it to the list and, eventually, members would be assigned to do it over a series of Saturdays. All the men and boys over fourteen were required to participate, though people whose skills were in work other than construction would sometimes be assigned other kinds of projects.

By putting in for the church's help, Dad was clearly not hiding his defiance of the rule of a "unified home." Hiding wasn't his way. If he made a decision, he stood by it. But word spread fast.

One Sunday not long after that, Dad went to give his tithing to Rulon. Grandfather looked at him and said, "Son, are you subdividing your house?"

"Yes."

"Why?"

Dad explained that his wives needed some privacy.

"How dare you!" Rulon thundered. "You must have a united house."

Dad shrugged. He knew that this would be seen as rebellion against the prophet—and a sign that he could not control his wives. Rulon had already chided him repeatedly for not "controlling" Felicia better. She regularly defied the dress code by wearing pants to work, cutting her hair short, and using nail polish. But Dad didn't care about those things. And he couldn't live his life caught between warring sisters. Peace at home was more important. Grandfather would have to deal with it.

But what Dad didn't fully realize was that Warren really had already taken total control. And he was gathering all the evidence he could find to make the case against Ward to Rulon, to ensure he wouldn't protest when Warren finally pulled the trigger on my father. Bit by bit, his arsenal was coming together. And dividing the house gave Warren another major weapon.

TWELVE

Calves in a Stall

Jeremiah's hands were shaking as he brought the eight-inch bowie knife to the cow's neck. The animal was many times his weight, but completely passive, trusting, despite being bound with heavy ropes to a huge tree. It just stood there with its big, dull eyes. Moments before, we'd seen Dee Jessop slit another cow's throat. Dee ran a small children's zoo in Colorado City and he'd brought these animals to Salt Lake with him.

As our eighth-grade class watched in complete silence, Dee had drawn the knife across the first cow's throat. He looked like Crocodile Dundee, wearing a straw hat, khakis, and a many-pocketed jacket. I guess that's how he thought a zookeeper should dress—it certainly wasn't what other FLDS men wore, though it had the required long sleeves and pants. Within seconds, the cow's blood streamed out and the dying animal slowly tipped over. For a moment, time seemed to stop. I felt dizzy.

We were in the compound, standing in a field, the green mountains

surrounding us. The willow tree to which the cow was bound was ancient, about three feet in diameter, tall and leafy. Girls—and even a few
boys—started screaming and crying. Some were vomiting. Warren was
inside the school: he never seemed to be around for things that took any
kind of courage. After the first cow collapsed, they brought another one
over and Jeremiah was selected to kill it.

He was one of the "good kids" in my class of about thirty kids. He
never acted up and always did what he was told. But unlike most of the
brownnosers, he didn't act like he was better than us and would sometimes hang out with kids like me, just as long as we weren't doing anything that could get him in trouble. He was tall and stocky, with a baby
face and light brown hair.

He looked terrified. He tried to copy Dee's swift motion with the
knife, but he missed the jugular vein or didn't go deep enough and then,
panicking, started sawing at the cow's throat. The animal was in agony,
lowing in unmistakable pain. Dee ran over to finish the job and then we
had to deal with the carcasses.

It was 1996. For the rest of America, President Bill Clinton's reelec-
tion campaign and the cloning of Dolly the sheep were the big news, but
for us it was the apocalypse. The world was going to end in four years or
less and we had to be ready, even the youngest children. During the
apocalypse there would be chaos, and only those who knew how to survive without the trappings of civilization would make it. So Alta Academy had to train us. I couldn't believe what Warren was making us do
now. And the timing of the end of the world was really pissing me off.

That morning, survival class had started with instruction on how to
catch, cook, and eat worms. The teacher—who was one of Warren's
brothers—took us outside and we found some, wriggling and dirty and
slimy. Then he put them in a frying pan, cooked them over a camping
stove, and made us eat them. They tasted like dirt—not slimy anymore,
but crispy. Although everyone was supposed to eat some, a few girls just
pretended and no one really pushed it.

Next, we moved on to chickens. They taught us to pull their heads
off with our bare hands. By this point, the girls were completely freaking out, and although the instructors tried to make everyone do it, some
kids simply refused and sat down and cried.

But the worst part—by far—was the cows. Once they were dead,

Dee and the other guy cut them open and started gutting them. The smell of blood was sickening, overwhelming. Dee cracked the skull open with a chisel and took out the brains. After he'd skinned one cow, he made me hold some of its brain and rub it along the inside of the skin. Something about the membrane around the brain was supposed to soften the skin—and he told us this is what we would use for our survival blanket. I had to keep my mouth closed to keep from throwing up.

I don't know why they thought we'd find cows or chickens to kill during the apocalypse, and it wasn't like a wild animal was going to stand there and let you tie it up and slit its throat or rip its head off. And wouldn't God ensure that His chosen people were taken care of anyway? Like everything else, it made sense only retrospectively—as yet another way the church leadership terrorized and controlled the people. By frightening us, they ensured we would obey unthinkingly, rather than considering how absurd their prophecies really were. It's amazing how well fear can work to suppress rational thought, something I unfortunately experienced over and over during my time in the church.

When they had finished gutting and skinning the cow, they took the meat away and cut it up for the families to eat. Then they released Grandfather's German shepherds. The dogs eagerly licked up the blood left on the grass. Pretty much everyone looked like they were going to be sick, if they hadn't already vomited.

———

Alta Academy had always been a strange school, but as Warren and Rulon's preaching reached a fever pitch in their obsession with the coming apocalypse, it got much, much weirder. We had about five "survival classes" when I was in eighth grade. During one, we had been made to sprint up the mountain, hard running, no stopping. It was serious exercise, like boot camp. When we got to where the trees were, the teacher went back down to help the girls and other stragglers who had lagged behind.

Warren did come with us for this class, and watched as his brother the survivalist taught us to put salt on a knife and hang it in a tree to attract deer. He said that deer had no feeling in their tongues, so they would come for the salt and just keep licking even as they bled to death. He also taught us how to make traps out of baskets of twigs for smaller animals, like rabbits and rats. We never caught any, even though he insisted that the traps would work when the time did come.

The hiking and hunting itself was pretty cool. I always enjoyed being up in the mountains. I liked learning about nature and how to live in it. It was definitely better than sitting in class listening to Warren.

But the constant talk of the end of the world and the increasing restrictions on what we could and couldn't do began to wear me down. It was exhausting, living with constant fear and threat. At home, we were supposed to be preparing for the end by stockpiling nonperishable food and other items.

However, with a family as large as ours, there was no way to fit supplies that would last for any amount of time in our pantries. Our grocery bills were already high enough. Anytime we did try to start stocking up, everything would get used up rapidly. We were warned that failing to be prepared might kill us, but it was impossible.

And, personally, I felt ripped off. I had to go through all these trials and troubles and yet—according to what they taught us—I would never get to have any wives or children. Unmarried men couldn't rule their own worlds or make it to the highest levels of heaven. We would be subjects of our dad's world, and I already felt like I had had enough of being bossed around by him for one lifetime, let alone an eternity.

In school and in church, they taught us that when the world ended, we would have to hide out in the mountains and fend for ourselves. God would swoop down, killing the unrighteous and making it seem as though all would be destroyed. Everyone else was the enemy: the wicked would be desperate and do all they could to kill us. We had to be ready for that, and fight to defend our lives.

Our small group would have to battle millions. By staying hidden in the mountains and living away from the dying American civilization, we would be safe until God lifted us up to heaven. He would save the chosen people at the end of the destruction, bringing them to Him while He cleansed the earth, then returning us to a revitalized planet and Zion. We'd have to eat worms and live off the land and face deprivation in the meanwhile, but we would survive while everyone else perished.

Still, it wasn't fair, I felt. I would have to deal with all that but never have my own planet, populated by *my* wives and my own celestial kids. I was just too young. I was supposed to be perfect and obedient, following all these complicated rules, yet I wasn't ever going to get the payoff we were all supposedly seeking. Worst of all, I would die a virgin. And that idea was really beginning to bother me because, as I now know looking back, I'd started puberty.

It seemed like one day I looked at girls and they were just girls—and the next, I couldn't stop watching them. Everything they did fascinated me. I wanted to be near them, but I didn't know why. And then my voice started cracking. I didn't know what was going on. Dad never sat me down and told me the facts of life or anything about what was happening to my body. I was growing and things were changing, but I was more confused than ever.

Around this time, my older brothers came home with a big brown bag full of porn magazines, which Brandon later told me he'd found down by the river. They showed them to me secretly, in one of their bedrooms. I was amazed. Pretty much all I'd ever seen before was girls in long dresses. Once, when I was younger, we'd spied on some girls from the neighborhood skinny-dipping in Little Cottonwood River—but while I'd been interested then, it was because it was something forbidden and because I'd gotten my older brothers to include me. I didn't really know why it was such a big deal.

Looking at the magazines now, though, I understood. I couldn't believe that was what women really looked like under all their clothing. Now I desperately wanted a chance to see—and, God, please, feel!—for myself. I had worked out the basic mechanics of sex, but it all still seemed weird to me. I wanted to know more, but I couldn't really ask anyone. The world was about to end, and all the adults would do was tell me not to think about sex anyway. It was my rotten luck to hit puberty during the end times.

Now, whenever I saw the girls at school, I couldn't help trying to imagine what each one looked like undressed. Warren had made this really difficult: now the poor girls had to wear long underwear under long pants under long dresses, which must've really sucked for them, too, especially during the crazy hot Salt Lake summers. Boys had to wear long underwear all the time now, too. And it wasn't the Mormon temple garment: it was regular long underwear as practice for when the true temple would be restored.

On the playground, when we played capture the flag, you'd get to tackle the members of the opposing team. This was a rare chance to have physical contact with a girl. So if a pretty girl held the flag, I'd maneuver so I could be the one to tackle her. Of course, she'd quickly yell at me to get off her. She'd been taught to treat me "like a snake" and that she was beautiful now "only because boys hadn't touched her," according to Warren. Soon he stopped us playing that game anyway.

We weren't even supposed to talk to the opposite sex. I began to understand the temptation Warren had preached about that had never really made any sense before.

"Here's the lesson for today, young people," he announced during one priesthood history class. "As you get older, as your body grows, you will be tested in this area of your life. I know that a child is tested very young in this. You have to come to loyalty and the love of priesthood, to where you'd rather die—you boys—than ever touch a girl and—you girls—you'd rather die than ever touch a boy or want to be touched, because once certain things are done, you cannot go to the celestial kingdom. You cannot go to the celestial kingdom if you get married wrong."

That was basically Warren's version of sex education: you should want death rather than sex outside marriage or a "wrong" marriage that wasn't arranged by him or his father. He kept on about this, always emphasizing obedience and not questioning the leaders. Every Bible story became a tale of how the obedient were blessed and the disobedient were cursed, no matter how much twisting it took to make the story fit the moral. Even thinking about a girl was "a great sin"—and God had killed people for it, he preached, giving what he said were biblical and Book of Mormon examples.

He said, "For boys and girls to join together, you are worthy of death in the eyes of the Lord." To protect ourselves from lust, he advised prayer and simply never being naked. "When you get undressed, even to cleanse your body with a bath, do it quickly . . . Consider that even your eyes should be guarded . . . You should keep yourself covered.

"In your daily walk in your home, you bigger boys don't go touch those girls, those little sisters. You girls don't touch those boys. You bigger girls, if you change their diapers, do it quickly."

Huh? I mean, okay, it made some sense that if you never got undressed, you could never masturbate. But getting turned on by your little sister or by changing a diaper? I now realize that this must have been an actual temptation for someone as sick as Warren. But at the time, it seemed ridiculous.

Besides, I still couldn't see why wanting to be with girls was so wrong. I kind of felt like I was a special case. I wasn't even going to be old enough to get married before the world ended, so I wasn't going to ever be able to be with a girl? If that was really true, why should I wait?

I continued to have my doubts about the religion, but with everyone around me caught up in preparations for the apocalypse, it became very hard not to take it seriously. All these drills and plans and the slaughter of animals made it seem so frightening—and so real.

————

Warren and Rulon preached that, because the apocalypse was coming, the people needed to be even more perfect and godlike to ensure their survival. This was the rationale for all the new rules. No television except for news. TVs were permitted only in parents' bedrooms. For kids, TV was banned outright. We weren't even supposed to watch *Nature* anymore, let alone sneakily laugh at *The Simpsons*. Even books—particularly children's books—were forbidden. The images in these books were idols. Kids should learn to read from the Book of Mormon or from Warren's approved writings. Unapproved books were publicly burned in Short Creek.

Movies were especially bad and to be avoided. Now Warren preached that even wholesome movies like *The Ten Commandments* were sacrilegious because they contained what he saw as "nakedness." And, of course, radio and tapes and CDs—except for Warren's hymns and speeches—were blasphemous and could get you in trouble if you were caught with them. Some people would listen to his sermons on tape throughout the day.

Jewelry—other than a simple wedding ring for those who were married—had already been banned. We were all wearing the damn underwear. One Sunday, Warren decided that the color red was reserved for Jesus, so now everyone had to throw away all their red clothes, toys, and other possessions. Warren even began to regulate church members' sex lives, requiring the women to track their cycles and permitting sex only during ovulation. If God's people didn't obey the prophet and his mouthpiece Warren, no one would be elevated and all would suffer.

And then, it got even stranger. Warren began preaching that almost all material possessions were "idols" and that we had to stop worshipping them. He wanted us to rid ourselves of worldly goods in preparation for the apocalypse. Anything that wasn't "useful" was a worldly thing. This included all kinds of trinkets, artwork, even family photos. In our family no one did much about this, but other people began selling or throwing away—or hiding—their most personal possessions.

I'd started taking woodshop class in about fifth grade. We'd make wooden boxes and other decorative items as projects. But when Warren started in on idols, that had to stop. One morning when I was in eighth grade, Warren preached that wall sconces were idols. When we went into the shop that day, the teacher was practically in tears. He dismissed the class and told us to play outside because he was afraid that anything he could think of to make might be interpreted as idolatry by Warren. That would get him in trouble, and possibly even lose him his wife and kids.

That had become a real concern for everyone. It was around this time that we began to hear about many "reassignments." In our family Vera had left on her own accord, but rumors started flying around the schoolyard about what was happening to other families. If Warren decided that a man wasn't "perfect" enough, he would reassign his wives and kids to another man and take the first guy's priesthood away.

Of course, it wasn't just the man who had to be perfect; his wives and kids were a reflection of him, so if they were out of line, that too could be reason for a reassignment. "If a woman rules over a man both will lose the spirit of God," Warren had preached. Having a rebellious wife or child was a sign of that.

And if a man lost his priesthood, this meant that he had no authority in the church at all. He had to go away and repent. If he continued to tithe and wrote a confession that Warren decided was appropriate, the prophet might readmit him and give him back his family. But probably not.

Warren claimed that people's failure to reach perfection was preventing the rest of us from being lifted into heaven. That was his only justification for destroying these families. Early on, it happened to only a few people, but when I was in the eighth grade, the pace escalated. Every day there'd be whispers in the parking lot about how this one got a new dad and that one's mom had been sent to Colorado City. Ultimately over 250 families were torn apart in this way.

During recess one time, a friend told me that one guy had lost his priesthood because he refused to make his family wear the now-mandatory long underwear. The "good kids" began to avoid this guy's son—who was in our class—because he was from a family that was now disgraced. This didn't seem right to me. That kid had just lost his father and his mothers now had to marry and bed someone else. Just because they didn't wear the right underwear?

Warren preached from the Bible and from the Book of Mormon that those who fear God should be raised "like calves in a stall" and that this would protect us. But was obedience to this kind of leadership wise, or were we too being led unwittingly to slaughter? Ever since Vera had left and my dad had split our house, the goody-goodies in school had been even more snobby toward me and my siblings. We were starting to be seen as a troubled family ourselves. Would Warren dare to try to take Dad's remaining wives from him? And if he did, what would happen to us?

THIRTEEN

Double Yoke

The infant-size white coffin was covered with green leaves and tasteful ivory blossoms, but nothing could hide the horror of burying a baby. The bright sunshine and cloudless sky only made us feel worse as we gathered at the gravesite. My parents' first granddaughter—Clayne's second child with his common-law wife—had died of SIDS. Cheyenne was only seven months old when her mother found her, unmoving, in her crib. Nothing could be done to save her.

We didn't know it then, but our family's responses to Cheyenne's death would provide Warren with the final evidence he needed to convince Rulon to take away my father's priesthood. Of course, my parents weren't supposed to have contact with apostates like Clayne—and they certainly weren't supposed to help arrange a funeral for his child at a nondenominational funeral home run by Gentiles or invite those Gentiles and apostates to our home to ease their grieving.

But Mom and Dad refused to let Clayne and his girlfriend mourn a child alone. That would surely be a greater sin. Clayne needed them and they weren't going to let some ridiculous religious rule keep them away. About a week after Cheyenne's funeral, they decided to hold a memorial for Cheyenne at our house. It was the Fourth of July, 1997, so it was sort of an Independence Day celebration, but no one was feeling especially festive. The idea was to ease Clayne's sorrow by surrounding him with family.

Dad knew that holding such an event for an apostate and inviting Gentiles into our home was strictly forbidden. Both Warren and Rulon had continued to intensify their preaching that if a family member had an "evil" or "foul" spirit in him, he should be cast out, so as not to "infect" everyone else. There was no message of forgiveness at all anymore: if your child was violating the rules, he should go and you should keep sweet and cut him out of your life as if he'd never been born. The church was becoming ever more inhuman.

We all huddled around Clayne, trying to offer some comfort. He looked as if all of the life had drained out of him. He loved kids and he'd doted on Cheyenne. She was his little angel. He was still struggling with drugs, but he was trying to be a good father. You could see that in his interactions with the little ones. That day, he was out of his head with grief. My brother David, Big D, was closest to Clayne, who clung to him quite a bit. I tried to do whatever I could think of to help, but the situation was beyond my range of experience at fourteen.

We were so sad for him, but since we'd been taught to hold our emotions in check, there was very little crying. What most people would think of as normal expressions of grief were stifled. Even in mourning, you were supposed to keep sweet and paste a smile on your face. After all, you'd be reunited in heaven—and you should accept God's will graciously. Yeah, right.

At some point, all of us went outside. It was another dazzling summer day. No one knew what to say or do so people kind of floated around. Then, someone noticed a figure up on the mountain, in an area where no one usually went. Curious, one of my brothers went inside to get binoculars. We saw a man looking back at us through his own! We soon concluded that this was a spy of Warren's, but what was he doing up there?

A ripple of anger went through the family as we stood there trying to make sense of what we were seeing. I couldn't understand how the prophet and his favorite son could be so cruel: Why would you try to deny a man who'd lost an infant the comfort of his family? Dad was trying to support my poor brother, who'd suffered the worst loss a parent can face. The family grapevine had surely informed Warren of the reason for the gathering—and Warren would have informed Rulon. How could anyone see this as a sin?

We were furious that our privacy was being invaded on such an awful occasion. I was filled with rage. That was the one emotion everyone in the family expressed.

We went down to the street with my dad. David and Clayne wanted to smoke a cigar. Although tobacco was frowned on by the FLDS, we didn't see it as a particularly big deal. Still, out of respect, we didn't do it in the house.

We were down by the driveway smoking when we saw Warren's car approaching. It was a black Lincoln Town Car with tinted windows and bulletproof glass. I think he was driving. There was no reason for him to be on that road: it led to nothing but a residential neighborhood filled with Gentiles. If he wanted to get anywhere—downtown Salt Lake, Colorado City, a store—he'd have to go the other direction.

The only reason he had for being there was to show that he'd caught us "sinning." He wanted us to know that he knew we'd violated the rules of our faith. Behind him was a car driven by one of the church elders—one of his enforcers, really—I guess so he'd have a witness. He stared at us again as he drove back to the prophet's house.

My brothers who were out of the church—Clayne, David, Don, Brandon, and Nathan—all stayed over for the weekend. On Sunday night, we lit some fireworks. The kids were enjoying them, bursts of color flaring like bright flames over the mountains. Dad was thinking about what had happened the day before, starting to process it. He knew that Warren was up to something, and the more he thought about it, the more likely he thought it was that he would be called into his father's office. He tried to prepare himself.

Although Rulon was still in possession of his faculties, Warren had already become very powerful. It started in earnest in 1995 or 1996. Rulon had already become frail and tired. Warren started speaking for his father, and soon anything he said was seen as his father's wishes, whether or not Rulon had actually been consulted. Grandfather never really stepped aside, he just gave Warren more and more responsibility.

Warren played it as though he was being helpful to his father, doing this and that because it was too much for Rulon. At first, these were the least important functions, but over time, Warren started making more critical decisions and Rulon simply didn't have the will or the energy to stop him or stand up to him when he disagreed with a decision or policy.

And, at this point, Warren was preaching incessantly that if you have wayward children, you must cut them out of your family. You have to cut them off: it's not your choice. If you have a bad apple, even one with just a tiny scar on it, you need to throw it away before it rots the rest of the barrel.

As my father puts it, "Warren was getting very black and white in the sense that if you had someone who is questioning loyalty to the prophet and his teachings, then for God's sake push him out of your family! Well, I didn't ever push them out. My boys chose to step away because they were gagging and puking on Warren, as I called it. Do you think I would ever turn them down if they called saying 'Dad, can I come over? Can I bring my family?'

"And I suppose it was a thorn in Warren's side that I would take this liberty on the edge of the compound. Because we lived on one end, we were not as visible, and our front gate accessed a public road, so my children could come and go, not necessarily having been observed by the rest of my family. But I never chose to hide any of that."

The call came the next afternoon. Everyone was still reeling from little Cheyenne's death, but an even darker pall seemed to drop over the household. Anxiety, pain, and fear blazed through us all, but no one knew what Rulon's summons meant. My dad's mood always set the emotional tone of our household and he seemed as stressed as I'd ever seen him. He was tight-lipped as he prepared to leave and walked through the gate that led to the prophet's house.

Dad went straight to his father's office and handed him a tithe check. Rulon accepted it. Then the prophet's demeanor became grave. Dad could see that his father's eyes were bloodshot.

"Son, I've got to tell you you've lost your priesthood," he said, without any preliminaries.

"On what grounds?" my father asked.

"For harboring Gentile children in your household."

Dad didn't deny it. He admitted that he had allowed David—who had run away, become addicted to drugs, then begged to move back—to return home. He conceded that he'd held the Fourth of July gathering for Clayne and his family.

"By doing so you've exposed your family to the ways of the world. We know that you're smoking, that your boys smoke who live with you," Rulon added.

"On the grounds of loving my children and helping them, I lost my priesthood?" my father said, still not quite believing it.

Rulon quoted scripture to justify his decision—or really Warren's decision, my father has no doubt. The prophet talked about passages which say that church members cannot carry a "double yoke." Like an animal with two masters, a person with a double yoke is pulled in too many directions at once. Rulon wasn't finished. He told my father that he could not carry the cloak of the saint and live the lifestyle of a Gentile. This wasn't godly—it was dishonest, a pretense. By allowing his way-ward children into his home, that's what Dad was doing. Dad was living a "life numbered among the saints" and trying to be in the world simul-taneously. And that had to stop.

"You've got to choose."

"Are you kidding me?" Dad said. "Are you making me choose be-tween my family and my church?"

Rulon nodded.

"Well, you know what?" my father said. "I'm choosing my family. Thank you, Dad, for all you've done." My father shook Rulon's hand quickly, stood up, and strode out of the room, hurt and enraged. Rulon kept the tithe check. And Dad knew as he left that a man he'd seen as an inspiration—his own father—had become corrupted. The way Dad saw it then, Rulon was now being led by the devil, not God. He had be-come a false prophet.

In one breath, my father was in the church; in the next, he was start-ing a whole new life. He chose to walk away from everything he was raised to believe, the church that had once been his entire reason for liv-ing. My father later told me that it was his experience in Vietnam, seeing the bravery of his lieutenant and the way this supposed Gentile had lived with honor and goodness, that allowed him to make the right choice.

He knew that there were good people outside the church and that the way he was raised was not necessarily the only way to God. Other men might think that the only way to heaven was to go off and repent and let Warren and Rulon reassign their families to other men. But not Dad. He had chosen to put family first by taking Dave back and sheltering Clayne while he mourned his baby. He wasn't going to stop now.

He came home and called everyone together. He told us that we'd been excommunicated for harboring Gentiles. Felicia and my older brothers who had left home couldn't suppress their joy. I think Felicia actually said "Yahoo!" or something like that. But my father and mother were crushed. They had wanted to practice their religion and pass through the gateway to the celestial heavens. And now the door was barred.

When we woke up the next day, there was a chain on the gate that allowed us entry to my Uncle Allan's yard, the parking lot, and the rest of the compound. My brothers and I were furious and took Dad's tools and broke the chain. That night, Warren ordered someone to weld the gate shut. When we woke up the next day, there was no way to open it without destroying the metalwork. Although we were dying to tear the whole damn thing down, my father ordered us to leave it alone and not play their game. Rulon called my mom and offered to assign her and her children to another man if she wanted to stay in the church, but my mother told him no. He didn't bother to ask Felicia.

I didn't know what to do. Part of me was with Felicia, cheering that we no longer had to live under the church's restrictive rules. But another part of me was convinced that I would be damned as an apostate and that I should find a way to stay in the church. My family seemed to be spinning in all directions. I began to think that maybe I needed to find my own way.

PART THREE

FOURTEEN

Short Creek

It was hard to believe that my parents were leaving the church—that they'd been transformed literally overnight into the worst kind of people, the apostates that church leaders always described as "filthy and low" and "living like animals." But there it was, plain as the welded gate at the end of our yard. Church members, even my close cousins, now wouldn't make eye contact or speak to us when we passed. I wondered what would happen to us, whether Dad would have to choose just one wife. I didn't know if I could handle any more conflict.

The thought of being cast out weighed heavily on me. Just before Cheyenne's funeral, I had become a deacon. I was sealed into the church with the solemn ceremony that most boys choose to undergo around age fourteen. At that time, if you feel you are ready, you ask your father if he thinks you are mature enough to enter the priesthood.

It means a lot because it marks your transition into the adult world and your entry into a brotherhood that has transmitted holy authority from prophet to prophet, going all the way back to Jesus Christ himself.

According to our church, men in the priesthood are the only people in the world who can receive revelations directly from God. This ability is passed through this lineage. When I'd told Dad I thought I was ready for this honor, he agreed and, as is traditional, he'd sought the prophet's approval.

With that granted, I had attained the first level of the priesthood in the one true church. In the ceremony, as the men of the church placed their hands on my head and prayed, I was given the first set of symbolic keys to my salvation; I was no longer a boy in the eyes of God and the church. In fact, in our theology I now had more decision-making power than any woman—even Mom.

If I rejected this legacy, I would be doing it as an adult—turning my back on everything I had been taught to believe throughout my childhood.

I was in shock and didn't know if I wanted to relinquish my birthright. I felt extremely guilty. I didn't want to live in hell for all of eternity. My brother Aaron had also decided to stay; he was living with our uncle David. My parents said they'd support whatever decision I made. I could see that my mom was sad, but I didn't know what else to do.

So when my friend Richie said I could live with him down in Colorado City, I decided to try it. I'd visited him and his family many times there before. He wanted to help me keep my priesthood; he didn't want me to leave the community. His father, Howard, would be my priesthood head, the role usually played by your own father. With some twenty-seven kids, Howard didn't think one more would be a problem. I could live with their family in good standing as a member of the FLDS. Maybe there I'd learn to be obedient and keep sweet and live up to the "royal blood" that supposedly ran in my veins.

I packed some clothes. Dad gave me a used red Yamaha Riva scooter for transportation while I was there. I hitched a ride in a semitrailer owned by some church members who had a shipping company. I hadn't spent a great deal of time in Colorado City, but the memories I had of it were good.

When I was about eight, we'd visited for the Harvest Festival, a celebration led by the prophet that expressed gratitude for the crops raised on nearby farms. The residents set up stalls, selling homemade donut

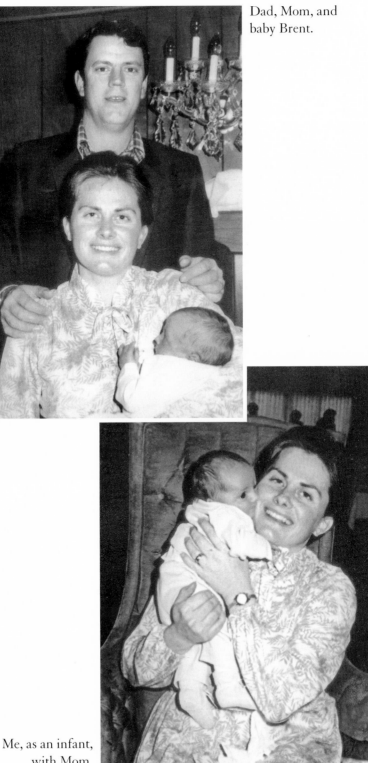

Dad, Mom, and
baby Brent.

Me, as an infant,
with Mom.

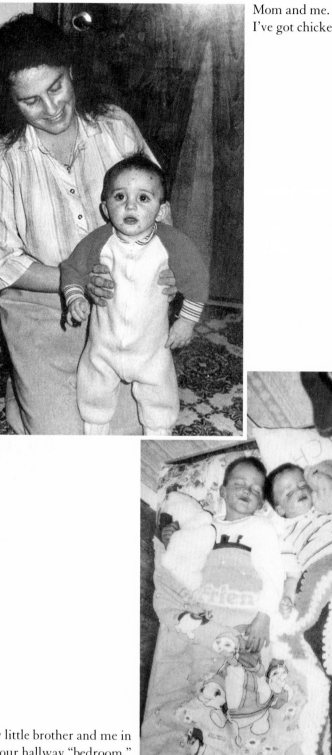

Mom and me.
I've got chicken pox!

My little brother and me in
our hallway "bedroom."

With one of my sisters, on Easter.

One child from each of my moms; I am between two of my sisters.

Mom, Dad, and most of us kids near the compound. It's a local tradition to paint on this rock.

All of the boys in my family know how to feed and change infants. I am on the right.

The men of the family, on Sunday before church.

Some of my best childhood memories involve the fishing trips my father took us on. I caught a pretty big one here.

ABOVE: Cheyenne's funeral.
INSET: Clayne and his daughter Cheyenne.

This is me, shortly after I first met Jody.

I get to kiss the bride!

Hailee loves to get her picture taken. Here she is with Jody and me.

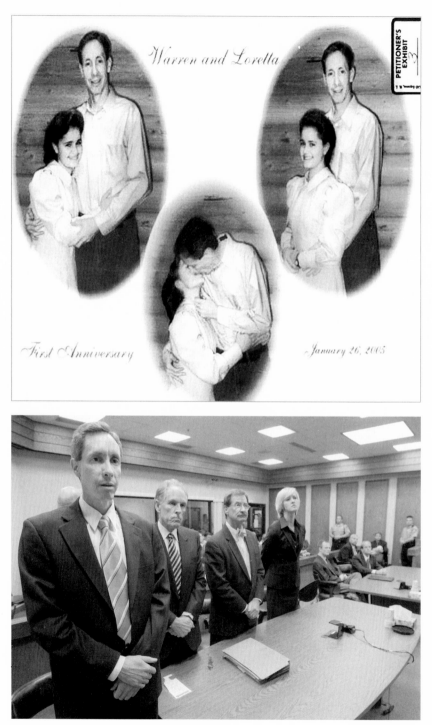

TOP: Warren Jeffs holding and kissing a young girl. BOTTOM: Warren Jeffs reacts as the verdict of guilty is read while he stands with his defense attorneys in the Fifth District Court on September 25, 2007, in St. George, Utah.

holes and other goodies and trinkets like little hand-carved wooden bears. Everyone was having a good time, and there were lots of things for us kids to do.

There was a little train to ride on and a park and lots of booths with games to play. It was the kind of family celebration that brought out the best in the church, that allowed us to be together and enjoy one another, rather than focusing on all the "thou shalt nots." Dee Jessop had set up his zoo there, and they had ostriches and elephants and a bear and all kinds of other animals that made a big impression on a little kid.

The landscape is dramatic, with the towering vermilion cliffs and wide open majestic sky. It's the kind of place that can't help inspiring religious thought, because man seems so small in the face of nature.

Another geographical fact about the place played a more practical part in our faith. The state line between Arizona and Utah bisects the town—the Arizona side is called Colorado City, the Utah side is Hildale. We still call it by its old name, Short Creek—or just "the crick." But the border has often helped the FLDS in its long-running battle with law enforcement over polygamy. State officials have no authority outside the lines of their state, and it's often been hard for either Arizona or Utah to prove that a crime like polygamy or underage marriage actually took place in its jurisdiction. According to one history of the FLDS, the location wasn't chosen for that reason—the twin towns supposedly grew because that's where the founders of our church owned land. The border sure was convenient, though.

I think Richie's family lived on the Arizona side—no one really paid much attention to the border. Howard had two wives—Richie's mom alone had nineteen kids and her sister-wife, who lived in a separate building on the same land, had over half a dozen. For some reason, this separate living arrangement was tolerated. Consistency is not one of the FLDS's strong points. With all his mother's kids, Richie's house was a jumble of random and oddly constructed additions. In the one where I stayed, you had to climb through a window from the main house to access the addition from within because they hadn't even built a door.

The addition was large enough to be divided into maybe thirty bedrooms, but it was completely unfinished. In fact, the window into the addition was usually kept closed because the place had no heat or electricity. Oh my hell, did I freeze down there some winter nights! Even the main house didn't have central heating, so we'd stay around the fireplace in the living room till it was time to sleep and freeze in the coldness of the addition, with only small electric heaters for warmth. These had to be used with long extension cords from the main house.

Richie's father, Howard, was a character—he wasn't like other FLDS men because he didn't take himself seriously. He was a jokester who made light of everything. One time he put Krazy Glue on one of his son's bike seats, leaving the boy with the choice of taking his pants off or staying a long time on that little bike. Another time, he sprayed black ink on a black phone in the house so everyone who tried to talk on it wound up with a black circle around one ear. He didn't have great social skills, so he'd often seem clumsy and weird. But he was respected because he was incredibly smart and could fix anything—from washers and dryers to cars, radios, and vacuum cleaners. Richie seems to have inherited both his father's sharp brain and some of his unusual attitudes.

When I arrived, Howard convened a family meeting to introduce me to everyone and then said a prayer to welcome me. Richie's brothers helped me take my stuff into the room I'd be sharing with him and everyone was really nice. It was a relief because I wasn't used to being away from my family for long.

Since I didn't have any money, I got a job shortly after I moved down there. Alta Academy had closed and Warren told everyone to homeschool their kids—but what really happened for a lot of teenage boys was that they dropped out and worked. At times in FLDS history, young men were assigned a "work mission" in which they labored for the church for a year or two, helping build houses and other buildings needed by the community. The boys were often called when they were just out of high school, but it could happen earlier.

I worked at an auto body shop run by some members of the Barlow family. We rebuilt tractors. I later learned that this was illegal child labor. I was doing sandblasting and working with dangerous equipment that a kid my age shouldn't even have been allowed near. I'd use a machine that sprays beads of sand all over the car or tractor; it peels the paint right off. It could also take your hand off if you weren't careful. But it paid for gas for my scooter and it kept me busy. And I didn't have to think about my future, which was helpful because I had no idea what to do next with my life or with anything, really.

Now that I was a deacon, I had to attend priesthood meetings every Saturday night at the Leroy S. Johnson Meeting Hall. The low, pale yellow building looked more like a warehouse than a church, but it was huge, if partially unfinished. Many houses in Short Creek were similarly incomplete, even shoddy looking. Some say this is done to make people look poor for tax and welfare purposes. Others say it's because of the variable availability of cash and labor to complete building projects by getting on the schedule for help on Saturday Work Days or from work missions. Either way, the towns look rundown and haphazard.

Priesthood meetings were held in the main meeting room, the same place as services. All the men of the community would gather there to testify and pray, talking about the priesthood role they held and their gratitude to be part of the church. They would first split into groups, distinguished by their hierarchy in the church. As the lowest ranking, the deacons were in the back, and the highest—the apostles and the prophet—sat on the podium.

My grandfather would open the meeting with a few words about being the prophet. He was sickly and required oxygen by this point, so he wouldn't say much more than "I am the prophet and I know this church is true and I'm thankful that all of you are here to adhere to all these teachings and take them home with you and share them with your families. Today I have my representative for me to talk. Here's Warren Jeffs."

Warren was then the first counselor, the highest of the apostles, which is the rank below prophet. He would express his gratitude for having that role in the one true church and then drone on as usual about perfect obedience.

He'd talk about how we should set an example for the younger kids by coming to priesthood meetings, giving our full tithe, and working hard on the Saturday Work Days. He'd go on about how we needed to follow in the footsteps of the holy men higher in the church. About once a month, he'd lecture about the sin of masturbation and how we shouldn't defile our body's temple. Like our church services, these meetings were extremely repetitive, stressing over and over and over the need for us to do as we were told so we could live the principle and gain the highest realms of heaven.

Soon a holder of the Melchizedek priesthood—the rank you needed to get married—would testify. Same deal, gratitude for having attained this priesthood and emphasis on the true nature of the church. Men would often share experiences that they believed showed God working in their lives. For instance, a guy would speak about nearly losing a hand to farm equipment or being able to rapidly get out from under a car when a jack had fallen and then say, "I know that that happened because I hold a key to this church and I have the power to communicate with God and He protects me and I know that the church is true."

After everyone who felt moved had testified, Warren would close the meeting with a prayer, thanking God for all our blessings and imploring Him to help us take what we learned to heart. Then came the most important part of the meeting, at least as far as Warren was concerned: the collection of the tithes. Everyone had to tithe at least 10 percent of their income, and we'd put the money in an envelope and turn it over to Grandfather on our way out.

Sometimes, those seeking favor would arrange a special meeting with Grandfather to tithe. They'd bring their sons to try to show them off to Grandfather, to have them noticed as upstanding church members so that they could eventually get wives. Often Grandfather was too ill to collect the money, so Warren would do it himself.

The first couple of times I went to the priesthood meetings, I felt welcomed. I was a man now, I was going to learn to play my part. I tried to pay attention and take heed. I thought Howard would be my priesthood head, but apparently Warren wanted to keep close tabs on me, so I was assigned to "report in" to someone higher in the church.

Reporting in was one of the many ways the church leadership monitored the members. Once a month, every man would report on his life and his sins to his priesthood head. Nothing was off limits. You had to tell everything, whether you'd smoked a cigarette or jerked off, or if you had talked to a girl. If you did something wrong, you could expect to be lectured about it. You knew that it would filter up to Warren if it was bad enough.

Women and girls didn't have to do this, but their husbands or fathers were expected to keep them in line and report any major disobedience or failure in "keeping sweet." This kept Warren and his henchmen on top of all the gossip and gave them material to use against you if they wanted leverage to keep you in check.

Of course, I didn't realize this back then—I thought it was just part of my religion. And I wanted so badly to be good and to do the right thing. Most of us did, and that was yet another thing they had on us. If you hold the keys to a man's salvation, it's very easy to manipulate him. I was also so wrenched from what had happened with my family that I wanted something solid to hold on to.

So I was trying to keep sweet in my new life in Colorado City. I was working, I was going to church on Sundays, participating in the Saturday Work Days, and trying to stick to the straight and narrow. As best a fourteen-year-old boy could, I was trying to be a responsible and reliable person.

But within a few weeks, I found myself messing up. The other men and their sons had learned by then who I was and what had happened to my family. Rumors and gossip spread rapidly in the community. When I walked into the next priesthood meeting, no one would initiate a conversation with me; they kept to the little groups they were standing in, and some even pointed and stared. I tried to say something to someone, but it was as though I was a stranger who'd walked into the wrong saloon in the Old West.

I soon got this kind of treatment on the street and in church as well—from everyone but Richie and his family, even the other kids if any adult was watching. They were afraid of being judged. It wasn't enough that I was trying; that didn't matter. I was still my father's son and Dad was now an apostate. My father's sins had been visited on me and no one but Richie's family would give me a break. The unfairness started to make me bitter. People were judging me for something I had nothing to do with and could do nothing about.

I also think there was some long-standing resentment of the Jeffs that was being projected onto me. For most of the history of the FLDS, the Jeffs had lived in Salt Lake and did not keep a close watch on Short Creek. Other families were more powerful there. But now, Rulon Jeffs was the prophet and he and his ambitious son Warren seemed to be moving their base of operations to the border towns—or at least, spending a lot more time there and building large homes for themselves. People in Short Creek had always had some suspicion of us "city folk," and people in Salt Lake tended to see those who lived in Short Creek as hicks. So I think this was another reason I was being excluded.

There was also temptation everywhere. Like most teenagers, I was obsessed with love and sex. I'd been an early bloomer—writing notes to a girl named Danica when I was in third grade. She never wrote back, but it didn't stop me and I can still remember her big blue eyes. I think I wrote "I like you and will you play with me?" I got in trouble, of course. Though we'd been taught to treat girls like snakes, even Warren's best brainwashing couldn't conquer human nature.

When I'd first arrived, Richie had introduced me to his friends. One day we were walking in town, just hanging around looking for something to do. I saw a beautiful girl walking by, and it turned out that he knew her. Like my third-grade crush, she was also blond haired and blue eyed. Something about her just melted me. Her hair was long and straight and her skin smooth, her features almost perfectly symmetrical. I introduced myself and told her I'd just moved in.

Unlike the adults of the community, she welcomed me. She told me her name was Lisa. I was usually really shy, but somehow I got the courage to tell her that I thought she was pretty and asked her to meet me that night at ten "out by the crick." I was deliriously happy when she said yes.

Meeting at that time posed a risk: there was a 10 p.m. curfew for everyone in the community and the local police—who were all members of the church—would patrol the streets looking for violators, especially teenagers. They acted under Warren's directives. If they caught you, they would lecture you, bring you home immediately, and wake the man of the house. Then most kids would be in serious trouble—risking a beating or grounding or worse.

I bought a single red long-stemmed rose from the market in Short Creek, which was owned by church members. I planned to tell anyone who saw me with it and asked that it was for a sick relative or for one of Richie's moms.

I had butterflies in my stomach as I watched for her under the moonlit sky. Although Short Creek ran through the center of town, its banks were sheltered by large maples, cottonwoods, junipers, and other tall, leafy trees and in many places by dense underbrush. Some of the cottonwoods were eighty feet tall and had massive trunks. It was wild, hidden, and beautiful down there, away from prying eyes. The creek bed itself was pretty much dry, with an occasional trickle of a stream after a downpour. But it was certainly a spot where people could go if they wanted real privacy.

Then I saw her. We greeted each other and I gave her the rose and a love note I'd written, saying that she was cute and made me feel good. I spread a blanket for us so we wouldn't have to sit on the bare ground. A huge smile lit up her face as she took the rose and read the note. For a while, we just talked. Soon I got up the nerve to put my arm around her and we cuddled. Then, magically, she turned, looked into my eyes, and kissed me. She initiated it. I was blown away. I'd never felt like that with anyone before. We made out for hours before we reluctantly decided that we had better sneak back home.

After that, we met there as often as we could—sometimes every night. Within a few weeks, Richie and Lisa's sister also started sneaking out to the crick with us, but her sister and Richie mostly just talked.

My scooter and the eight dollars an hour I was getting at the body shop also gave me a taste of freedom. I would drive three miles to a gas station called Canaan's Corner, which wasn't run by people in the church. I'd slip the attendant an extra ten dollars to sell beer and cigarettes without IDing me, and I'd be the coolest kid in the crick, smuggling these forbidden items to our secret hideout. Somehow, Colorado City wasn't taming me.

Although the mainstream Mormon church forbids use of all intoxicants, the FLDS has sometimes turned a blind eye to alcohol. We had alcohol in our house growing up and the prophet even had a hidden wine cellar. I can't imagine Warren didn't sneak a few drinks from time to time. In fact, Dad says he heard about at least one time when Warren and some of his brothers in their teens got completely wrecked. I know for sure that my grandfather drank. In fact, you could probably call him an alcoholic. He always had at hand a big glass with a lot of clear liquid in it. My dad later told me it was vodka. Lots of men and women in the church seemed to "keep sweet" with a hand from Jack Daniel's.

I'd gotten drunk for the first time on peach schnapps that my brother Dave had stolen from my parents when I was around thirteen. He gave it to Nathan and Nathan and I downed the whole bottle, and soon we had the spins and were throwing up all over the place. Dave—who was much older and had moved away and then back home briefly—was laughing his ass off at us.

I started smoking cigarettes with Richie, who thought it was cool. Though I liked how it looked to smoke, I never really got addicted; in fact, the next year I had some sort of allergic reaction to cigarettes that put me in the hospital for five days. After that, I didn't smoke cigarettes again. But down in the crick, I did, wanting to look cool in front of my new girlfriend.

Lisa didn't smoke, but she would drink beer with me. I understood by then how alcohol could take the edge off, and it helped me be less shy and open up with her. In fact, Richie and I began to throw parties that made us hugely popular with the other kids. They started shortly after I arrived. But we were too scared to do it more than three or four times. We'd found a spot up in the mountains that was perfect, however.

Many of the people in Colorado City kept horses; one of our neighbors had about a dozen of them. After work, Richie and I had an arrangement with these neighbors: we'd help clean and feed the horses, and in return we were allowed to ride whenever we liked. I'd never been on a horse before, but I slipped into the saddle that first time and took to it pretty naturally. We discovered a horse trail that led up into the mountains, out behind one of our neighbors' houses. And that's where we threw our first party.

I spent my whole paycheck on $150 worth of beer—it took me six trips on the scooter to Canaan's Corner and back to carry all of it. I still don't know how I didn't get caught: I was fourteen and driving a scooter laden with beer back into town. But I did it—and then we used someone's red Radio Flyer metal wagon to get the beer up the mountain.

Earlier that day, Richie and I had ridden our horses up the mountain to scout the best place to make a bonfire. The redrock mountains had plenty of boulders and cliffs that could hide our activity from those in town who might look up there. We made sure our spot was secluded and then dug a pit and placed stones in it, like I'd seen my dad do at home. We told our friends and they told theirs, and that night we had forty kids up in the mountains, drinking and partying. I sold the beer at a small markup to earn back my paycheck. No one minded paying.

And we sat under the starry sky, poking at the fire, trying to make sense of the universe—but unlike other teenagers, we were faced with an unusually baffling set of practices and paradoxes. We had been told the end was near, but was it? We wanted something more than this life of dread and preparation, but we didn't know what. Everyone got drunk. When Richie and I decided to go home at about around two in the morning, there were about a half dozen kids passed out on the ground. We had to leave them to fend for themselves.

Lisa came to the party, of course, but she didn't want to fool around that night. She wanted oblivion. Like me, she had problems with her family that weighed on her. When she wasn't thinking about those issues, she was bubbly and funny, making everyone laugh. But that night she wasn't her usual effervescent self. As we drank, she told me more about what was going on.

She said that her relationship with her father was bad and getting worse. The constant fighting made her miserable. I tried to make it better, but I didn't think there was anything I could really do to help.

FIFTEEN

Butterflies

Not surprisingly, we'd had no sex education at Alta Academy. Warren gave his lectures against masturbation at the priesthood meetings, explaining that it would lead us down the path to premarital sex, which was, of course, even worse. The lesson was always just say no. So all I knew about sex was what I'd cobbled together from my brothers and from seeing those porn magazines they had found by the river when I was about twelve. We had managed to keep them hidden for a while, but then Benjamin's mom walked in on him when he was helping himself out with one. She threw a shoe at him and made him burn every one of them.

My parents never told us anything about sex either. At school, all we heard about was obedience and the sacred principle of celestial marriage. What you were supposed to do once you had all those wives wasn't to be discussed. It was just another thing that didn't make sense to me.

When I thought about my feelings for Lisa, I felt that freethinking part of my mind come to life. How could someone choose your life part-ners for you when you felt so differently about different girls? How could the prophet possibly know who you would love, who made you feel butterflies? And how could you leave such an important choice to someone else? It just didn't feel right—and I definitely couldn't imagine sharing my girlfriend with anyone else. The very thought of it made me furious. How could women like my mom stand it? I could see that my dad didn't feel the same about Felicia, Mom, and Vera—why would God want such a thing?

These questions were all very unsettling and Lisa and I took things slowly. For weeks, we spent most nights together, just fooling around and talking before we had to sneak back home. Over time, we went fur-ther, but before we went all the way, we talked about it a lot. I didn't want her to do anything she would regret. After all, we'd been taught that girls should prefer to die rather than lose their virginity before mar-riage. It's hard to explain just how big a deal they made of it. It was like we were living in biblical times. I did not want to make her feel dam-aged or ruined.

We were completely terrified of pregnancy. Fortunately, I did know about condoms. I'd found one on Dave's dresser just before my parents were excommunicated. I asked what it was and he explained it to me. Before I even thought about having sex, I got some from the store where I bought my beer. Our first time was what I now know is the usual mix of awkward and awesome. For days I could think of nothing else.

Of course, we dreamed about running away, but we couldn't see the idea as more than that. Leaving the church together wasn't something we could get our heads around. We talked about it more than a few times, but we were just fourteen. Where would we go, how could we support ourselves? If we were only a bit older, I told her, I would have married her and left.

But as it stood, her father would surely sic the police on us if she es-caped—and there would be nothing I could do about it. She was under-age: I could even be charged with statutory rape, though I suspected that wasn't very likely since I was only fourteen myself. And this was the irony: if we got caught, she almost certainly would be immediately married off to an old man, someone with high status in the church like Warren. Then she would be raped repeatedly, and I wouldn't be able to stop it.

I'd seen this happen to others. One girl who came to one of our parties had been caught sneaking back into the house by her father. Shortly thereafter, she was married—to one of those older men. Any girl who was either pretty or rebellious or both risked this fate: the men knew that once a girl got pregnant, she wouldn't want to leave her child and would be even further bound to the community.

Warren even hinted at this obliquely in one of the "dictations" he later sent out when he went into hiding. He said, "Great is our Heavenly Father, taking care of these daughters of Zion at a young age so they and the boys will not go through the troubles of immorality and social evils among us."[1] That's right—he claimed to believe that marrying teen girls off to old men was "protecting" them and the boys from the immorality of premarital sex. In reality, underage marriage was a sick way to control women. The threat of it terrified the girls and kept them in line; the fact of it trapped them by tying them down with children. And, not incidentally, it satisfied the lusts of perverts like Warren.

This fear was very real for Lisa. One day her father caught her returning home after a night with me. He raged and told her that if it happened again, he would arrange her marriage. She said she'd refuse. She railed and screamed back at him. But her fear increased because she didn't know any other way of life. Like me, part of her believed the church was the only path to salvation. And though we kept meeting, our times together got shorter and she became ever more cautious.

————

I would wait for her every night. Sometimes I'd wait an hour before I realized that she hadn't been able to sneak out and wasn't going to come that night. Her father became increasingly suspicious, but she worked out plans with her sister to distract or avoid him so that she could come to our secret hideout.

Ultimately, we got busted. I can't remember exactly how it happened, but her father blew up and took her out of town to a trailer that was miles from civilization. I certainly couldn't see her there. When she got back, she wasn't allowed out unaccompanied even during the day. I was devastated: I would try to catch her eye when I did see her, but it was clear that it was over because there was simply no way for us to meet. We couldn't get around the restrictions her father had placed on her. I was miserable. It was definitely one of the reasons I ultimately left Short Creek.

Richie's mom also busted us once, when we came in drunk and smelling of cigarettes at four in the morning. She told Fred Jessop—who was the bishop of the church in Colorado City—and we had to go see him. He lectured us about how bad what we were doing was. It was worldly. If we wanted to live a happy, fulfilled life in the church, we needed to be obedient and stop drinking, smoking, and talking to girls.

Richie and I sat there and nodded and told him what he wanted to hear, but we had no intention of stopping. It was like I had a split personality. One part deeply believed everything I was told by the church and believed in hellfire and brimstone; the other part insisted that my religion made no sense and that the things I wanted to do were normal, teenage fun. In a split second, I could go back and forth—holding completely opposite positions and not even noticing the contradictions in my thinking or behavior.

After Lisa was sent away, I began to turn away from the church more seriously. I went to services only because Richie's mom woke us up every Sunday morning and it was easier to go than argue. But like I'd done as a kid in devotional in Salt Lake, I started sneaking out in the middle of the prayers. Some boys would leave one by one to go watch TV in someone's house—or even play video games that someone had smuggled in from the nearby town of St. George. Colorado City was a ghost town during services because everyone else was at church. We could smoke right out in the open and do whatever we wanted because there was no one around to stop us.

I also started lying about participating in Saturday Work Day projects. Because Richie's dad was Mr. Fixit, Richie and I were often assigned to help him on his rounds. We'd lift appliances and do other things to make his work easier, rather than working on the usual construction jobs. But then we began to lie and tell him that we had weekend jobs in St. George. That kind of thing was allowed as long as it brought in more money for tithing.

Instead, we'd go there and hang out with lost boys who had left the church and their friends from the neighborhood. They would have wild parties where dozens of kids would be packed into a small house or apartment, blasting hip-hop and getting drunk. Some kids would be throwing up in the bushes, others were smoking pot and taking painkillers. The houses were absolutely filthy, with cigarette butts and beer cans everywhere and all the furniture pretty much trashed. I thought it was really cool that they could have girls over whenever they wanted, but there seemed to be something desperate about it, too.

I began to drink really heavily now. I missed Lisa terribly. I could have had nearly any girl I wanted in Short Creek. Some of them were throwing themselves at me, I guess because they saw how well I had treated Lisa. But I didn't want them. I wanted her. And the more I thought about it, the more the whole principle of celestial marriage began to bother me.

Even when I had been with Lisa, I had had opportunities to fool around with other girls. For me, however, being with someone was about caring for them. I didn't want sex just for its own sake, and I didn't have the kind of feelings I had for Lisa for anyone else. I didn't want to cheat on her because I knew how much that would hurt her, and I certainly didn't want her to do anything like that to me.

I just didn't see how you could manage more than one relationship without the favoritism, jealousy, and fighting that I'd seen more than enough of in my childhood. I'd visited Mom's parents from time to time as a child—her father was also a polygamous prophet—and his wives seemed okay living together. But I had no idea what went on behind closed doors there. Sure, it might be cool to have many different girls, but as Dad once said in exasperation, the work and pain for all involved wasn't worth it.

Now when I went to the creek or up into the mountains for a party, my goal was to get as blitzed as possible. The only way I knew to handle feelings was to drown them, ignore them, or pretend they didn't exist. Alcohol made that a lot easier. I would guzzle beer and talk with Richie about the church and how things seemed to be getting more strict, more controlling, and more strange. One day I finally said that I couldn't see myself staying much longer. He agreed that he couldn't imagine a future for himself in the church either. But for the time being, we were still too scared to do anything about it.

Then Richie's mom caught us again. She had begun checking our beds at 11 p.m. every night. For a while, we got around that by waiting until after she checked and then leaving. But that night, something went wrong. We came in at 3 or 4 a.m., completely drunk, laughing and falling over, and she was standing in front of my bedroom door. "What do you think you're doing?" she demanded.

"We're going to bed, we're tired," I said.

"You smell like alcohol. Are you drunk?"

At that point, I just went into our bedroom and lay down. She was his mom—Richie could deal with it. He just said, "Yeah, Mom, we're wasted," and slammed the door in her face. She stormed downstairs, saying he was in big trouble and that she would tell his father.

The next morning, she wouldn't even look at him. "You two disgust me," she said, and started to preach to us about how evil we were and how wrong it was for us to drink and be disobedient. We were sent to talk to Howard, who was outside, fixing some appliances.

"I hope you had fun," he said. We'd known that he had gone through his own rebellious phase as a teen. He definitely didn't take our misbehavior as seriously as his wife did. He asked us if we'd been drunk and we admitted it. "Yeah, I got an earful from your mom last night," he said to Richie. "The church forbids drinking and I don't condone that and I don't want you guys doing it anymore, so please don't." And that was it.

Around the same time, Howard decided to play one of his jokes on me. He took the fuses out of my scooter, temporarily baffling me as to what was wrong. When I figured out what had happened, I went to him and he told me that Warren had called him and told him that Richie and I were "behaving immorally" with girls.

Apparently, Lisa's father had told Warren about us. Howard insisted that I'd have to go meet with Warren to discuss the situation. Until then, he said, I didn't deserve the scooter. That part was not a joke. I retorted that my dad had given it to me—and that I was going to ride it anyway. He refused to return the fuses, so I hot-wired it with tinfoil and drove to an auto parts store and replaced them. He didn't try to stop me riding it after that.

But now I had to meet with Warren. I wasn't afraid of him at that point. I had put the memory of what had happened when I was little out

of my head. I certainly didn't expect being alone with him to be pleasant, however. I thought about not going. But the obedient side of me
won out, dragging me down to his office.

———————

By this time, Warren had really abandoned our compound in Salt Lake
City, as he and his father prophesized that the great destructions would
hit hardest there in the new millennium. His new home in Short Creek
took up an entire city block. It was surrounded by high-tech security
cameras and walled off from the community—you had to be buzzed in
and then pass through a series of magnetic security doors. The house
echoed his sense of privilege and high position.

I was to meet with him in his church office, in the meetinghouse. It
was also well defended by security cameras and magnetic doors and
clearly designed to be intimidating, with a massive custom-built
wooden desk.

Warren was seated behind that desk, glaring. He stood up and shook
my hand limply. Hatred and anger welled up inside of me. I wanted
desperately to wring his ugly chicken neck. My posture was defiant as I
listened to him lecture me about *my* immorality, *my* lack of obedience,
my failure to keep sweet, and *my* pending damnation.

He said that I was going to wind up like my family—as an apostate
with no hope of salvation. He tried to talk big to me, but I looked at him
like, whatever, dude. I had no respect for him and I think he could see
that in my eyes. I also think he was somewhat intimidated by me. I
wasn't in first grade anymore. I was strong from hard labor and bigger
than he was, though not taller. Still, he went on with what I now saw as
his godly act, droning on about the consequences I would suffer if I
didn't repent and stop sinning. He kept at it for a good twenty or thirty
minutes while I just sat there silently fuming. Finally, he ran out of
steam. He said it was good meeting with me and he hoped we'd meet
next time on better terms. I said good-bye and walked out.

And that was it. I felt nothing. I thought it was bullshit. I didn't re-
vere him as a prophet, I couldn't stand him. One of the biggest regrets of
my life is that I didn't kick his ass that day. But that was the final shrug
for me—I had had it. I needed to figure out what to do next.

After the meeting, I went back to Richie's house. He wasn't around, so I bought some beer and cigarettes and went down by the crick to think. I knew that it wasn't working out for me with the church, but I didn't want to abandon Lisa. I really loved her and it tormented me that I couldn't do anything to help her because we were just fourteen. Running away with her wasn't going to change that. She was too damn young—old enough to be married in the church, but not old enough to get away from it.

Then I thought about my family and how they had been treated. My brother had lost a baby—a seven-month-old innocent baby. My family had been excommunicated for trying to do what any real human being would see as the right thing. They'd been raised in the church for generations and had spent decades of their lives and given thousands of dollars and hours upon hours of work supporting it. They'd risked arrest by practicing polygamy. And what did they get for it? Bitterness, fighting, and ultimately rejection.

I realized that I belonged with them. I went back to Richie's and called my mom. I said I was sorry that I had left and that I had been confused. I asked if I could come home. Mom, of course, was delighted. I told her I needed a few weeks to wrap things up and would arrange to return home with a trucker, the same way I'd left. I wanted to say good-bye to Lisa.

Soon I managed to meet her sister in the grocery store to tell her what I had decided. Fortunately, both their parents were out for a few hours that day and both sisters were home, minding the kids. Lisa's sister agreed to babysit by herself while Lisa came out to meet me. We went to our usual spot. I told her that I was really sorry, but staying in the church was just not working for me.

She agreed; she felt the same way. "I hate the church, I hate my dad, I hate my family, I wish I could leave."

I felt awful. "I wish I could do something to help you. I don't know what to do."

She looked at me with love and said, "I understand, it's fine. I'm happy for you. I hope you can be happy up there with your family."

I said that if she ever wanted to run away, if she ever needed anything, she should just call me. I gave her my parents' number and I told her that I still loved her and that all she had to do was call and I would pick her up. "That's about all I can offer at this point," I said. We hugged and kissed for a little bit, and then she went home. She was too scared of being caught to make love one last time. I hoped for years to get that phone call, but it never came.

SIXTEEN

The Chronic

I sat in the school assistant's office, shaking uncontrollably. She was try-ing to show me where my classes were on a little map of Albion Mid-dle School. I was terrified because I still wasn't sure that coming home and giving up the church had been the right thing to do. Now here I was, surrounded by Gentiles at public school. The sermons I'd heard about how evil and corrupt outsiders were and how apostates like me would burn in hell were running through my mind yet again, even as I tried fruitlessly to concentrate on what she was trying to tell me.

Although my parents had been excommunicated, we still lived in the compound. One of Dad's brothers had made a humiliating lowball offer on the house, but my father had refused to take it. Daily life at home hadn't changed that much since I'd been in Colorado City. Dad was still married to both Mom and Felicia and the house was still split.

The main difference was that now we were shunned by those of our cousins and aunts and uncles who still lived in the compound.

I was afraid that the Gentiles in school—especially the kids—

wouldn't be much friendlier. We lived in an affluent neighborhood and all the kids streaming by seemed to be dressed in designer clothes. I was wearing a borrowed T-shirt from one of my brothers and some ancient hand-me-down jeans. I knew I stood out, but I had no idea how to fit in.

All my life, I'd had to dress as a plyg kid. On the bus to school that morning, I'd heard that word whispered. I sat up front because I knew that the kids in the back were the same ones who sometimes threw ripped-up porno magazines and water balloons into our yard or drove by yelling "plyg." The bus driver would shut them up if they started anything he could hear. I was bigger than almost everyone on the bus, so they weren't likely to try to beat me up—but they sure didn't seem to want to befriend me, either.

I didn't know what music these kids liked, what styles were popular, or anything about what was cool and what wasn't. It was overwhelming. Although my younger siblings Adam and Miriam also went to Albion, we were all in different grades so that didn't help much.

"Are you okay?" the assistant asked, seeing how anxious I seemed. I tried to explain that I'd been in private school for years and that I wasn't good at talking to new people, but I just wasn't able to express why I was acting like I was facing a firing squad, not ninth grade. So she just laid out my schedule, showed me where everything was, and walked me to my first class. She took me up front and introduced me to my teacher.

And I felt everyone's eyes on me. I knew they were thinking, "Who is this weird kid?" I felt they could see through me and knew where I'd come from and judged me for it. It took all my strength not to run out the door and never go back.

I had to throw everything I'd ever been taught out the window and try to put on this face of a normal kid in society. I was still shaking wildly. It seemed like an eternity before the assistant left and I could sit down. I went straight to the back of the room and dropped my schoolbag. I put my head down on a desk and closed my eyes. I was struggling to get control of myself and just freaking out.

For at least the first week, I came home and cried every day. No one spoke to me and I didn't know how to act. Every day I battled my own mind about hell and damnation and Gentiles. And every day I faced kids who seemed hostile—or indifferent, at best. I told my mom I didn't think I could do it. "No one likes me, no one talks to me," I kept saying. And she told me to give it time; I had to go to school.

Although it seemed to take forever, I did start making friends after a few weeks. The preppies and the jocks and the kids with the nice clothes and cars still wouldn't have anything to do with me. The brown-nosers and the goody-goody Mormons weren't an option. But the stoners accepted anyone. And I was happy to join in the activity they liked best.

The first time I'd smoked pot was with my brothers. Clayne and David had gotten an apartment together and one by one most of my older brothers had moved in. The steady stream of their sons' leaving as they hit their mid-to-late teens had saddened Mom and Dad, but they had been unable to stop it. I started going to my brothers' apartment on weekends when I got back from Colorado City. One time they had tickets to a boat show and Clayne had this huge bag of weed. He must have been dealing at the time and I guess they thought I was old enough to try it.

I took a few hits off their bong and my heart began racing. I felt paranoid before we'd even gotten out the door. I was a nervous wreck. We went to McDonald's and bought all this food, but I couldn't eat it. I even threw up because I was so anxious. I should have stayed home, but I didn't know any better. The weed was so strong, I was seeing halos around everything.

When we got to the boat show, which was in a huge convention center in Sandy, they were laughing and falling all over one another. I was sure that everyone was staring at us and that they all knew. I got so spooked, I climbed into a big boat and sat there. They were having fun because they were used to it, but I didn't know what to expect or how to calm myself down. So I just waited and kind of hid till it got less intense and they got me out of that boat. Then we went back to their apartment and watched movies. I liked the feeling I got from pot, but at first I enjoyed it only when I was in a safe place and didn't feel exposed.

Soon after that, I met a kid in school who really liked to get stoned. He was one of the first kids who reached out to me. He was curious about my background but not judgmental. He thought it would be cool to have a lot of wives and started asking me a few questions about it. I tried to explain that it wasn't quite as cool as it sounded. He wanted to be my friend and invited me to hang out after school.

He lived with his father, who had divorced his mom and always seemed to have weed. Pretty much every school day, I would tell my mom I was going to do homework with my new friend and we'd sit in his basement and get high. He stole the weed from his dad, but his father never seemed to discover that anything was missing. If he did, he never said anything. His little sister had a crush on me and she'd try to hang out with us. But she was only fourteen and I was afraid I'd get in trouble, so I steered clear.

My friend was really into hip-hop, which I had started to listen to when I snuck out of Colorado City to go to those parties in St. George. We would smoke a bowl and listen to Dr. Dre and Eminem and Snoop Dogg, music I still love. 2Pac's *All Eyez on Me* or Dr. Dre's *The Chronic* made us feel daring and illicit. I liked the beats and actually didn't much listen to the words—but the fact that Warren thought black people were the devil incarnate didn't hurt in attracting me to rap music. We'd sit there—two white kids, one a perplexed former fundamentalist Mormon—and listen as gangsta rap spoke to us in raw emotion. We felt a lot of anger, emptiness, confusion, and rage, even though we had obviously had quite different experiences. Smoking da chronic made us feel connected.

———

Of course, getting wasted all the time probably didn't help my grades. But it wasn't my memory that was the main problem I had in school. There were huge holes in my basic education. I knew no science or history whatsoever. And I had no idea where what little I'd been taught about those subjects deviated from accepted knowledge. I didn't know what I didn't know.

One day one of my classes focused on dinosaur fossils. The teacher was explaining how they were discovered and what they could teach us about the history of the earth. He had curly brown hair and glasses and looked like a tree-hugger, the kind of guy who came to Utah to embrace nature. His hair was a little long and he dressed more casually than the other teachers, like an archaeologist on a dig. He was talking about the different kinds of fossils and what kind of evidence they provided about the development of ancient life. His explanation was quite different from the one I'd been given by Warren.

After class, I went to talk to him. I told him that I'd been taught that the world was made of a blend of earlier planets and that dinosaur bones were remnants of these prior worlds—not evidence that dinosaurs had roamed the earth. He was drinking a can of pop and he literally blew it out of his nose he was so convulsed with laughter. I could see that he felt bad for having embarrassed me, but he was unable to stop cracking up.

"Who taught you that?" he sputtered as he tried to compose himself.

I explained that I had been raised in a polygamous group and attended their school. I felt really stupid and ashamed. But he went over the material, starting from the basics that I had missed and explaining how scientific evidence works. He didn't think I was dumb.

He said that, in science, you begin with the simplest explanation that fits the facts: in this case, that the bones people had found were evidence that dinosaurs had once lived on earth. He explained how scientists determined how old the earth was and what that suggested about life. A light went on in my head. I thought, "Holy cow! That actually makes sense."

After that, I spent a lot of time talking alone with teachers. I told all of them about my past. I didn't want to embarrass myself in front of the other kids by asking questions during class. But from that day on, when I didn't understand something, I would ask afterward and they would provide the background that I had missed. I found that I actually enjoyed learning about science and history—about inventors and explorers and other great figures who had shaped the world.

When I read about Thomas Edison inventing the lightbulb or Christopher Columbus discovering America, I could see how they had affected the real lives of millions of people. It wasn't like being told about some obedient prophet who supposedly did something miraculous that probably never really happened. When we learned about the tectonic plates and how all the land masses had originally been one, you could see how the continents fit together, like a puzzle. You could prove—or disprove—this stuff, and there were particular methods to tell whether things were true or false. It wasn't just based on someone's say-so. You didn't have to take their word for it and you could think for yourself about whether it made sense or not.

That helped give me confidence as I struggled with my fears about having left the church. Those prophets weren't all that great. What did they really do, anyway, compared to someone like Albert Einstein? He was the kind of person who really made a difference in our understanding of the world. After a while, I too started to laugh at the stuff I'd been taught—it was some funny shit. But that took a long time.

I ended ninth grade with a 2.5 average. That wasn't so bad given that I'd missed years of work in history and science and was getting stoned all the time. By the end of the year, I had pretty much adjusted to being in school, although my social life was still quite small and limited.

But life at home was getting harder and harder to take. My mothers were still battling each other. Sometimes Felicia's kids would complain about something Mom's kids had done and Felicia would try to get into our side of the house. We'd lock all the doors. She'd pound on our front door, screaming to be let in. Finally, my mother would come down and tell her to get the hell away. Now that my family was no longer in the church, there was no real rationale for the sisters to live polygamy. There was no road map for a situation like this: without the church's guidance, there were no rules.

Their whole lives had been devoted to the "principle." It was supposed to take them to heaven. Without the FLDS structure, they foundered. Even though for years it was clear that their marriages weren't making Mom, Dad, and Felicia happy, they didn't know what to do instead. They had been raised to be obedient, but now they had no one to follow. What resulted was an even more intense power struggle between Felicia and Mom. Felicia had always wanted Dad all to herself—and now, as she saw it, there was no real reason she couldn't have that.

Dad's PTSD also intensified as he tried to retain control over his family. In some ways, he acted like he hadn't really left the church. He was the family patriarch and we all had to follow him. There were more chores than ever to do, and almost as many rules. He wanted me to work and give most of what I made to the household fund. He wanted me to do what he wanted when he wanted it, without question. But I was a teenager now and naturally chafing at any attempt to rein me in.

One weekend I decided to stay the night with my brothers and the next morning he called me up, furious.

"Where the fuck are you?" he demanded. "What the fuck do you think you're doing? We have shit to do. Get your ass over here—*now*."

He was so loud that I held the phone away from my ear and all my brothers heard him.

It wasn't worse than any of the other times he'd exploded at me. I knew he was under incredible strain and, looking back, I can see how hard this time must have been for him. But I just couldn't take it anymore. There was going to be one more Jeffs lost boy. I went home and had Brandon pick me up the next day when Dad was at work.

SEVENTEEN

Dazed and Confused

Brandon peeled out, burning rubber as we left the driveway. His car was fast and the speed was liberating as he drove us away from the compound. The Mustang had previously been used for highway patrols; now it was helping me escape. The sense of freedom I felt was like a million pounds had been lifted off my shoulders. I couldn't restrain my joy.

I couldn't stay a second longer; I needed to find a place in the world and understand the strangeness of the place I'd come from, the incredible power of our community, religion, and leaders to shape our lives both for good and ill. Only then could the pain that my whole family suffered mean something more.

We drove down the steep, twisting roads from the mountain into the flat Anytown, America, of strip malls and tract housing that is suburban Salt Lake. Brandon was soon taking me through the small two-bedroom apartment that would now be home to five Jeffs brothers. I would be sleeping on the floor, later moving up to the couch.

All I had with me was a duffel bag filled with clothes, most of them useless hand-me-downs. I was sick of them—and of being told what to do, of having every single part of my life regulated by my religion or my father. From now on, I would wear what I wanted, not what they told me I had to. I would be my own man.

I didn't realize then how hard it would be to make my own choices. I really didn't know how to live or move through the world or what was expected of me. I'd barely even ordered for myself at a restaurant; I'd never bought any of my own clothes.

When I was a child, no one had ever asked me what I wanted to be when I grew up. That was for the prophet to decide—we weren't encouraged to have our own ideas about it. I'd never daydreamed about being a fireman or a movie star or a basketball player like most kids do; my future was in God's hands, so wishing for something that might not happen would only court disappointment. No longer called to be one of the prophet's chosen people, I hadn't the vaguest idea what I wanted.

After Brandon led me inside, I sat down on the couch and looked around. It was unnerving not to have anything I had to do, no one to report to, no priesthood meeting or church service or Saturday Work Day to attend. I wasn't used to the aimlessness of not being in school or work or church, not being at the mercy of my dad's moods, not having to worry about what I was going to say.

Part of me liked it, but the other part was filled with fear. That old fear of eternal hellfire, endless pain, and damnation, the fear that I had turned my back on God. It sat there in the pit of my stomach, not going anywhere. Leaving home had brought it back again—just like starting ninth grade.

I considered going back for a moment, but then said fuck that, it's time to party. I sat in our small living room with four of my older bros. Brandon handed me a Bud Light. At the time, he was eighteen and worked in telemarketing. My half brother Nathan was the same age. He cracked open another beer. Nathan's much more emotional and high strung than Brandon, with light brown hair and rust-colored eyes—6' 1" and a bigger build. He and my brother David, who was twenty-one, worked in construction.

Big D had been the one who'd insisted I was welcome, who told me to move in anytime, despite how crowded the place was. As we toasted my new freedom, he said he was glad that I'd finally joined them. And I could see that he meant it, even though there really were too many people living there already.

Clayne, then twenty-five, worked as a server in a restaurant. Though I didn't know it when I moved in, by then he had started selling cocaine and was using heroin. He had become involved with some extremely violent dealers. Dave was also using hard drugs, but they tried to keep that stuff far away from the younger brothers.

It was a roller coaster living with my brothers. I was excited, then scared, all the time. My first few weeks were a blur of marijuana smoking and drinking. Although I didn't realize it at the time, the "lost boy" label was pretty accurate. Like Peter Pan's sidekicks, we had never really grown up. We'd been trapped in our own sick but also sheltered never-never land and were completely unprepared for what faced us in what now passes for American reality. So we got high.

At first, I was afraid even to go out of the apartment alone. It wasn't just paranoia from smoking pot, although that might have added to it. And it wasn't because the apartment was in a bad neighborhood. The building was in serious need of a paint job and many of our neighbors did not seem as though they had legitimate sources of income. We heard lots of shouting and even gunshots from time to time.

But even that really wasn't why I was afraid of going out by myself—it was more that I felt exposed and self-conscious, almost as if I'd come from another planet. I didn't know what I was supposed to do in the most basic situations, like going to a party or club. I had been dropped into a new culture, with little idea of the unwritten social codes. In my first few months out, in fact, I came across as a real weirdo.

I'd go to the Cottonwood Mall with my brothers and they would go up to girls and I'd freeze. I didn't know how to approach them and I didn't know what to say, and when they came over to me, I'd just stand there and stare. I don't know what they must have thought was wrong with me.

I guess I was afraid I'd be faced with experiences or questions that would make me look stupid and reveal that I didn't know things a guy my age really should know. I didn't want to look like a chump. So I stuck with my brothers—going out mainly with them, rarely alone, observing everything.

Safely back in our apartment, I would sit on the couch thinking about my life, trying to make myself calm down. I spent a lot of time zoning out, watching TV. Mostly, that kept me occupied. But then the fear would overwhelm me again, and I'd think about damnation and be terrified about my decision to leave and scared, too, to go back.

You could never know if they would take you back, of course—that was up to Warren. You might confess and repent and still be shunned. And who knew what God's judgment might be? The fear overwhelmed rational thought and consideration—it was paralyzing.

My brothers would sit there and tell me that what I'd been taught wasn't true, that the church was wrong and that I'd be okay. Brandon, especially, told me not to take that stuff seriously. He'd sit with Nathan or me or whoever was freaking out and just insist over and over that it would get better. However, at times it didn't feel like I'd ever fit in.

But after about a month, I got sick of being poor and decided to get a job. I'd never before worked with Gentiles in the outside world—only for church businesses, with their child labor and low pay and questionable safety standards. I was almost certainly in more danger doing sandblasting in Colorado City, but I was more scared now because I didn't know what to do working among strangers.

Nathan found a place for me at the construction company where he worked. I was a "rover," the lowest man on the totem pole. My job was mostly cutting wood to frame houses and doing what the other guys told me to do.

Fortunately, they trained me before I began work, so I didn't have to figure out safety practices on the job. Even so, I was still so afraid of the boss and shy with coworkers that it took months before I could bring myself to talk to them directly about any problems I had or materials I needed, rather than having Nathan speak for me.

The job did mean that I had my own money, however, and I began chipping in on the $700-a-month rent. I spent most of my first paycheck on new clothing. My brothers took me to the mall and I bought a pair of

Lucky jeans, an indigo blue Billabong T-shirt, a yellow Fox Racing shirt, and a red Lucky brand shirt.

That was all I could afford because those clothes were so expensive. But it was the first time I'd ever chosen my own clothing and worn something that wasn't a hand-me-down. I was styling.

———

However, now that I'd left my parents and was no longer distracted by fighting with them and by their fights with each other, I began to be overcome by confusion. I had never had to make my own long-term plans before. I hadn't been taught to have dreams of a different way of living, one that I could control. I'd never thought about what I wanted to do with my life or what its purpose was.

Much of what I'd been taught in church had been completely crazy, but there were also things that I deeply valued in my upbringing. It was hard to know what to keep and what to throw away. I had to choose a new set of values and ideals, but your values guide your choices in the first place. How do you choose new ones without being influenced by the old ones, which you now question? It was dizzying.

I'd never really had a chance to develop my own interests either. Drugs filled some of this void: I could smoke chronic and listen to rap, and there were things that went along with that that told me what to wear and how to behave. But I was still haunted by fears and doubts that the church was right, that I'd made a huge mistake and was now bound for hell, no matter what I did.

At some point, Brandon started taking me to nightclubs with a big group of his friends, letting me use his ID. The first time, I was so scared that I wouldn't get in I memorized everything on his ID. Of course, the bouncers didn't even really look at it—and so there I was in this huge, dark, crowded room with hundreds of kids. In the parking lot, before we went in, we pounded Bud Light and shots of Jägermeister because you had to be twenty-one to drink but only eighteen for admission.

I'd never been anywhere like that club. The music was pumping, techno and hip-hop, heavy on the bass. Lights were flashing, the floor was throbbing. Brandon had a group of about thirty friends, and they gradually made their way up to the stage, dancing. I kind of hung back and watched as he went behind this girl and started bumping and grinding on her. She didn't slap him or push him away—she went along with it. After a bit, I saw a pretty blond girl and I tried to do the same thing. We wound up dancing till two or three in the morning and I got her phone number.

It took about two weeks to get up the courage to call her, but I did and she agreed to go to the movies with me. I'd never had a date before, so I was really nervous. One of my brothers lent me his car. When I went to pick her up, I was so shaky I felt I had to explain, so I told her it was my first time living on my own and that because of that, everything was kind of new to me.

I didn't want to tell her about the church because I was afraid it would freak her out. Afterward, we went to a diner called Dee's Family Restaurant. I took her on a few more dates, but I didn't really feel a connection with her so I just stopped calling.

My work schedule was one of the few things that gave my life form and consistency. I gained confidence over time and stopped having Nathan speak for me. I got to know some of the guys and then the boss. But that brought a new set of problems: my boss started inviting me to get stoned with him every day. The first time, we were framing a house in Salt Lake City.

We went over to get something from the truck—Nathan, the boss, another coworker, and me. My boss said, "Let's smoke some bud." I didn't want to seem uncool, so I agreed and we all got high.

The rest of that afternoon, I had no motor skills. I could not keep my mind on the job. I was supposed to be operating an electric saw and all I wanted to do was sit down somewhere and eat. Being stoned and cutting wood was not my idea of a good time! I was afraid I'd slice a hand or an arm off. The noise made me anxious. After that, the boss would always offer me marijuana and I felt unable to say no. I didn't want to get him mad.

It was an important step for me when I could finally say, "Dude, it may work for you but it ain't working for me. I'm struggling over here and working really hard. I'm just way too high."

He said, "No problem, man, it's your preference" and that took the pressure off. I was so used to either being a drone and doing what I was told or completely rebelling and not doing anything. Being able to tell him how I felt took some strength. It was one of the many skills I had to learn to function outside the church.

So many lost boys stay lost because they can't do that. They don't really know how to negotiate these kinds of situations and make their needs known at work or at home. They stay in unhealthy relationships or job situations—or behave irresponsibly because they don't know what to do other than obey or disobey. They can't find a middle ground because they have never been taught to think for themselves.

Their drug problems escalate because they have a hard time saying no or avoiding situations in which the issue will arise. Unfortunately, I've seen this happen again and again to my friends and at times to some of my brothers.

Unlike many lost boys, I was lucky to have my older brothers and some other key people in my life show me the way. When Felicia had worked cleaning houses, one of her employers had been a kind, elderly woman named Sandy. She did not belong to our church but lived in the neighborhood. When I met her, she was probably in her sixties and used a wheelchair. She lived on her own in a big rambling house. Her husband had left her and she had several grown children who visited only rarely. Her main companions were her two Siamese cats.

Brandon got to know her first: I think he stayed in her basement when he first left home. Now we started doing some odd jobs for her around the house. She would ask us how we were doing and I found that I could really talk to her. She would listen and not judge. I told her why I left home and described my relationship with my dad and the struggles I had with the church.

She found the conflict in our family heartbreaking and infuriating. She was disgusted by the way the church split families apart. She thought my parents should have done more to help us boys—we were still teenagers and yet we had no financial support from them at all. I told her that compared to most of the lost boys, we were extremely fortunate. Some of them never saw their parents or siblings again; my brothers and I at least had each other and Mom stayed in contact.

But Sandy could see that I was having a hard time. She wanted to help. One of my biggest problems was that I relied completely on my brothers for transportation. I couldn't afford a car. I was just sixteen, so

I was too young to get a loan. "Go out and find a $4,000 car and I'll buy it for you," she said when she realized that having my own wheels would make the most difference for me.

I was blown away. I tried to tell her that she didn't need to do that and that I wasn't telling her my problems because I wanted something from her.

"I insist. You're not going to get out of it. I'm going to buy it for you anyway," she said every time I tried to tell her no. I finally said I would pay her back if she needed me to and I did more work for her. I bought a white Volkswagen Jetta and it did make my life a lot easier.

For a while I'd spend every Sunday with Sandy, just talking and helping her around the house a bit. She had done me a huge favor and I wanted to do right by her, but I enjoyed it too and it felt good to make her feel less lonely. She helped me to understand people outside the church, and to figure out what I wanted and who I was. I could talk to her about most things and I only hope I helped her half as much as she helped me.

About a year after I'd moved in with my brothers, Clayne and his girl-friend moved in together and the lease on our apartment ended. I began a period of bouncing around from place to place. I got a lot better at meeting girls and hanging out with them.

In fact, I found that girls really loved lost boys. Unlike many men our age, most of us actually wanted commitment. We looked for fre-quent contact and connection. We didn't want casual sex. We didn't play games. We even wanted to get to know their families. Lost boys didn't complain about hanging out with Mom and Dad or going to fam-ily functions. Indeed, we actively sought them out. We were unlike any other boyfriends they had ever had. Fear of settling down was definitely not our main issue.

A lot of women also liked the idea of rescuing someone. So many of the guys I knew who left Short Creek actually got engaged very quickly after leaving the church.

Of course, we were awkward at social functions at first—and as a re-sult, some guys got engaged to pretty much the first woman who would go out with them. But unlike other men, they were happy to hang out with the in-laws and aunts and cousins—in part, I think, because they wanted to replace the big families they had grown up in.

And though I had my brothers, I did miss my dad and our whole family, despite all the fights. I didn't know it then, but around this time Clayne and Felicia were working on something that would begin to mend that rift.

EIGHTEEN

Family Values

"Nothing I did was ever good enough," I told Dad. I could see him struggling to control his anger, his urge to argue and defend himself. But we were in what I imagine was probably the largest and most complicated family therapy session Jan had ever conducted.

She was a warm, motherly presence: her brown hair and build looked very similar to my mom's. We were seated in a plain room at the VA hospital, around a large conference table: Dad's two wives and Clayne, Don, David, Brandon, Nathan, Patricia, Benjamin, Linda, and I.

Clayne had set the event in motion. He'd read or seen something about PTSD and it clicked for him: this could be what was wrong with Dad. The bouts of anger. The distance. The hyper-vigilance and rapid changes in temper and mood. All of the symptoms he'd read about—plus, of course, the fact that Dad had seen combat in Vietnam—seemed to fit.

He went to Felicia because he thought that she was the person that Dad was most likely to heed. He told her what he had learned. She agreed that it was worth exploring and they arranged a time to talk to him. Felicia and Clayne gave our whole family a great gift by doing this.

When he heard what they had learned, Dad thought that what they were saying made sense. He agreed to go to the VA hospital in Salt Lake to seek help. And after a few months or so in therapy with Jan, she decided that some family sessions might not only aid his recovery but help all of us reconcile. Mom had called everyone to arrange it, so now here we were.

The ground rules were that we could talk about anything that was bothering us or had hurt us in the past and that Dad had to listen, not argue or use anger to silence us. Jan started by explaining the symptoms of PTSD and how it affects veterans. When someone is in combat, he is fighting for his life. The fear that this produces automatically generates anger: when you think about it, the two feelings aren't that far apart.

If you've ever seen a cornered animal—or someone in a car accident reacting to the person who hit them, even if fault is hard to determine—you can clearly see this relationship. When flight is impossible, fight is the first response. Anger gives you a better chance of survival. But this high level of arousal floods the body with stress hormones.

And it's difficult for the body to simply turn off these responses when you get home, whether it's from a war or any other traumatic event. The experience of extreme stress puts people with PTSD on a hair trigger. Afterward, even the tiniest threat is enough to flood the brain and body with stress hormones. This makes sense if you think about it from a survival perspective. Reacting quickly can save your life.

But being hyped-up like this all the time is not a pleasant experience. It can make vets with PTSD irritable and aggressive. In fact, if they experience emotions or sensations that remind them of their trauma, they may react with aggression and violence before they are even aware that they have done so.

The lower part of the brain can actually trigger this kind of behavior in a way that is really hard for people with PTSD to control. Again, this is useful if you are in a situation where it is kill or be killed, but it can wreak pure havoc back home, particularly in your relationships. I learned a lot more about this later when I realized that I too suffered this disorder.

In therapy Dad learned all about PTSD and how to manage his

anger better. He had uncovered the triggers that set him off and learned how to avoid them or calm himself if he encountered them. I realized that this meant that many times in the past, when he'd reacted with anger to his family, we hadn't been the real targets.

He hadn't meant to terrify us the way he did—it was part of him that had worked in combat but wasn't so helpful in civilian life. Jan told us she knew that many of us had left home on bad terms with Dad, and she hoped we would use these sessions to clear the air and restore our relationships.

Clayne spoke first—I think he made a joke about being the "most fucked up." He said that he was glad that Dad was getting help and that this itself was all he needed from him now. Dad and Clayne had reconciled earlier. But Clayne had a very hard time trusting therapy because of his bad experiences as a teenager. He was also ashamed because he hadn't been able to kick drugs, so he mostly listened.

Next each brother in turn talked about how Dad's anger had affected him. All of our complaints were pretty similar: his rage had terrified us and we didn't feel we could come to him for support or advice. Dad's face got red and he couldn't restrain himself from arguing back quite a few times, saying that if we'd just been obedient and done what we were told, we wouldn't have set him off. But Jan was in firm control of the session and she always brought the focus back to us.

As I listened to my brothers, it amazed me how much Dad respected Jan and accepted her guidance. I could see that he really wanted the best for us—because the easy thing for him to do would have been to refuse to participate. But he stuck with it. Watching him, I began to understand for the first time how hard our way of life must have been for him, too.

Growing up, I'd never thought that much about the level of stress he'd been under, with three wives and twenty children always wanting his attention and love. With memories of the horrific experiences he'd had in the war haunting him, it was no wonder he was often angry. As a kid, I was naturally focused on my own perspective. Now I could see Dad's side, too.

Nathan used the therapy to confront Felicia as well, telling her how she had made him feel worthless—that her constant screaming and focus on everything he did wrong had really hurt him. She, too, tried to argue, but again Jan said that this session was for the kids to air their complaints so that we could just get everything out in the open.

When it was my turn, I didn't say much that was different from what my other brothers had said. I'd felt ignored. I felt I wasn't able to live up to what Dad wanted from me and that made me feel awful about myself. Again, Dad tried to justify himself, but Jan reminded him that he needed to listen. He did, and so did Mom and Felicia.

I wasn't sure that therapy would work, but over the five to ten sessions we had, we really did clear the air. Our relationship didn't become perfect, but now we had one. I was proud that my dad had gotten help and I even went for a few sessions alone. I told Jan about how lost and confused I felt, and how I didn't know what to do with this life outside the church.

My childhood had made me wary about family life, and I had no idea what kind of work I wanted to do. I didn't feel that I really knew how to have a relationship with a woman and I felt aimless, purposeless. At least when I'd been in the church I knew where I was going. Now I had all the fears of hell—but no promise of any kind of heaven.

It's hard to explain just how strange it is to lose your community, most of your family, and an entire belief system and way of life. It's often hard for outsiders to see why people live the way my family had, but there are certainly advantages to certainty. While I had often felt lost in my huge family, there was no doubt that I truly belonged to something greater than myself, that I had somewhere I truly belonged. Now I wasn't at all sure where I fit in. And my life reflected my aimlessness.

I'm not quite sure of the sequence of events in this period, but at one point I lived in a completely chaotic house with my brothers in Sandy. We were selling large amounts of marijuana and so there were people coming and going all the time.

At that house we had constant parties, with lots of drinking and loud music. There always seemed to be someone crashed on the floor, always some kind of drama. I had to leave there because it became way too chaotic for me. It was just not how I wanted to live.

The problem was, I still didn't know how I *did* want to live. And I would soon learn that Clayne had decided to answer this question in as negative a way as is possible.

NINETEEN

Losing Clayne

The woman's voice on the other line was so soft and indistinct, I couldn't hear who it was. I was at Mom's house, so it could have been any of my sisters or half sisters or even Felicia. But it didn't sound like any of them. A wrong number? The woman was obviously distraught and sounded desperate. As I paced in the den, surrounded by the tan leather recliners that dozens of children and grandchildren had climbed on, Mom was moving around in the kitchen, preparing lunch. It was January 2002. I had been spending what up until then had been an ordinary weekend afternoon with my parents.

The voice continued in an agonized, repetitive mumble. And then all at once, I realized who it was and what she was saying. Her Vietnamese accent got stronger as she went on. It could only be Clayne's wife, Han.

"Clayne killed himself, Clayne killed himself," that's what she said. "He has a gun and he killed himself."

I froze. Clayne was the father of four kids by then and stepfather to one. He was only twenty-nine. He had a gorgeous wife and his two children with Han were just toddlers. I said I'd be there as soon as possible, hung up, and hustled Mom and Dad into their minivan. I told them the bare facts that Han had conveyed but that I still couldn't accept.

At the time, I was the only one of my brothers who was still close with Clayne. No one in the family had told me to cut him off for being an addict, but pretty much everyone else had backed away. Even I had put some distance between us: a few months before this, he'd come to me with a desperate story about how Han and the kids would be out in the street if I didn't give him money to cover his rent.

I signed over my whole paycheck—and of course he bought heroin with it as soon as he got the cash. I'd been furious with him, but I couldn't let go of my big brother entirely. Although I didn't know then how much we had in common, I must have felt it in some way.

Clayne and his previous girlfriend had had two children together. But their relationship hadn't survived their daughter Cheyenne's death from SIDS and Clayne's ongoing addiction.

After they broke up, Clayne had met Han in a bar where he had been working as a bouncer. She is petite, with glossy black hair and full lips. He wanted her the moment he saw her. Ironically, Clayne had decided shortly before he met Han that he wanted a calm, submissive woman who wouldn't argue with him. He'd had enough drama. He had that stereotyped view of Asian women, so he thought Han was the answer to his prayers when she came into the club.

As it turned out, Han is really a spitfire, with a feisty temperament that sometimes clashed with Clayne's more easygoing nature. Nonetheless, they had fallen in love. He'd even converted to Buddhism and married her in a Vietnamese Buddhist temple in Salt Lake. Clayne seemed to find some real comfort in the religion she'd been raised in. He'd been a bit scared to tell my father that he was falling in love with a Vietnamese Buddhist, but when he did, Dad said that if he truly loved her, he should marry her. My parents had never really embraced the racist beliefs of our church in the first place and they now rejected them entirely. But Clayne's marriage, unsurprisingly, had been deteriorating because he remained unable to kick heroin.

About six months before he died, Clayne had seemed to have a break-through during addiction treatment. He had been going to rehabs since he was fifteen. But most of them—particularly Provo Canyon School—had simply abused and humiliated him. The last time he was in treatment, he had been at the LDS Hospital for a slow inpatient methadone detox.

The psychologist there decided to try hypnosis, believing that his symptoms were so severe that he had to have suffered some kind of childhood trauma. Although this way of using hypnosis is controversial because some people have recalled false memories under its influence, what Clayne recalled was unfortunately all too true. Sadly, when he left treatment, although he was no longer ill from heroin withdrawal, he didn't have the means to cope with what he learned there.

Under hypnosis, Clayne revealed that Warren had raped him repeatedly when he was about kindergarten age. Two of Warren's brothers had been there, standing guard at the bathroom door. Sometimes the brothers had actively participated in the assault. My parents had always wondered why their oldest son had become an addict so young and why his condition seemed so intractable. They'd spent thousands of dollars on many different types of treatment, going into debt because insurance wouldn't pay for all of it. Now, finally, there was an explanation, hideous as it was. Mom and Dad were shattered by the news.

Clayne had recalled these memories in detox—in the voice of the five-year-old boy he'd been at the time. The hospital had called my parents in for an emergency family session. The psychologist who had done the hypnosis helped Clayne tell them. My mother felt as though she'd been shot through the heart.

At one point, she sat Clayne on her lap—her fully grown oldest son, the one who had given her so much trouble, the one she never seemed to be able to help—and held him while they all cried. It was the worst possible feeling for a parent, the sense of being unable to ease the pain of your child combined with the feeling that you should have been able to prevent the hurt in the first place.

Then came the rage. Both of my parents wanted to eviscerate and annihilate Warren and the brothers who had concealed and enabled his crimes. My father was serious. He would kill Warren and torture his two brothers for either making it worse or standing by and doing nothing.

But Clayne insisted he didn't want "blood on Dad's shoulders" because he didn't want him to go to prison and he unable to raise his family. About six of his children were still living at home, with Mom or with Felicia. Clayne made Dad swear to him that he wouldn't murder Warren or harm his brothers. He didn't want the past to destroy any more of our family than it already had. He felt guilty enough.

Mom sunk into despair. Her children were her world. Her job was to protect them. How could she have failed to see what was going on with her own kids? And how could her church have condoned such evil? Certain incidents now haunted her. The times Clayne soiled his pants, when he was around six, and Felicia had fits about it but Mom had just cleaned him up, furious with Felicia but getting no explanation from Clayne. The trip to the hospital when Clayne was peeing blood and no medical cause could be found. Warren hadn't been content just to rape Clayne—he'd tortured him in unspeakable ways. It wasn't bearable; it wasn't even conceivable. How could someone do such things to a child? To her child. My brother.

Before Clayne got out of the hospital, Mom and Dad gathered my full siblings together to tell us what had happened. They wanted us to understand Clayne better, to have more sympathy for him.

My memories of this time are incredibly fuzzy because I was hit with one disaster after another in the space of six months or so. All I remember from this gathering is that I was horrified and that I thought it explained a lot about Clayne's life. I didn't yet understand the relevance it would have to my own. I still spaced out when anything threatened to bring back my past.

And even though everyone tried to support him when he came out of detox, Clayne continued to fall apart. The memories ate away at him. He rapidly became re-addicted to heroin, which he was injecting. He sold more cocaine to support his habit, despite being in debt to dealers for hundreds of thousands of dollars because a shipment had gotten stolen before he went into treatment. Everything went downhill. Even now that he knew what had happened, even now that his self-destructiveness had a logical explanation, he still couldn't forgive himself.

He just couldn't find a way to integrate what had happened and live without anesthesia. He felt it was too late for him. He blamed himself for becoming addicted, for being unable to forget, even for having been abused, though he knew that that made no sense. He hated himself for not being a better father to his kids, for not being able to stop using. But life was unbearable for him when he did. There was just too much pain.

A few months before Clayne died, I went fishing with him and his family. Fishing was one of the few things he still enjoyed besides heroin. Outside in nature was one of the few places where he found peace. He took me aside, purportedly to go smoke a bowl. He told Han we were going farther upstream to fish. He sat next to me in this canyon by the river and began to cry silently. He said, "I have something I want to tell you. I don't want you to freak out or anything, but I have to get it off my chest."

I said, "You know I'm here. Whatever you need to tell me, I'll listen."

He didn't go into much detail, but he did talk about how he'd been molested by Warren, saying that it was important to him for me to hear directly from him about what had happened. He said that Warren had done things to him that I couldn't even imagine. "It took a part out of me that I never really got back," he said. As he said that, I could see for a moment the child he had been—not the broken man he was now. I was overcome with sadness. I felt that familiar feeling of being out of my body.

I was blotting out my own thoughts so I could try to help him. I couldn't bear to see how much pain he had inside. I wanted so badly to be able to do something for him, but like my parents, I was powerless. Clayne seemed completely lost. I'd never seen him so far down. I said the things you say in those situations, but I felt like I just couldn't reach him. Because he was the big brother whom I had idolized, it felt even worse.

We were both hidden behind such complex armor to block out our feelings that it was impossible to get through. My own memories didn't come back then. In some ways, I wish they had so I could have told him and maybe he wouldn't have felt so isolated and ashamed.

But both of us had fought so hard to keep those memories down, we could deal with only a tiny bit at a time. So after that short, intense conversation, we just fished for a few hours, smoked some weed, tried to lighten up a bit, and went back to Han and the kids.

By the time my parents and I arrived at Clayne's small two-bedroom apartment in downtown Salt Lake, the police were everywhere. Han's mother, a tiny Vietnamese woman who spoke no English, was trying to calm her daughter and grandchildren. Clayne had apparently gone into the bathroom, fired at the wall, and then, before anyone else even knew what was going on, shot himself in the head. Han—trailed by all of her family—had raced into the bathroom after she heard the first shot. They'd all seen his ruined body and the blood-spattered walls. They were deep in shock.

The police tried to stop me from going in there. They told me about how suicides usually fire a test shot first, to see if they can take it, and only then fire the fatal shot. But I just couldn't believe that Clayne was dead. Even though it made no sense, I was sure I would find out that it was a mistake, that someone else had shot himself in Clayne's bathroom. I pushed past them and now have written on my brain forever a sight no one should ever see. Of course, it was Clayne lying there.

Time slowed down. I felt like I was moving underwater. I tried to prevent my parents from getting into the bathroom and seeing him, but that was about all I could think of to do. I couldn't believe that I had lost my brother and that Warren was still out there, leading the FLDS, living a life of privilege while destroying so many lives around him. I knew I had to do something, but it would take another trauma before my own history unfolded and I figured out how I could help.

My trauma resulted from a mistake Clayne and I had made a few months before he died. He was going to meet one of his drug connections, a guy I can only describe as a kingpin. Clayne asked if I would ride with him, and I said yes. I had no idea where we were going, otherwise I wouldn't have even considered it. We drove up to an estate with stone lions guarding a gateway to a long driveway. For some reason, he decided that it would be okay for me to come inside with him, something he should have known better than even to suggest. I think he must have been beyond caring by this point.

We walked up the driveway past the fountains to a huge, imposing home. There were marble columns at the front. It was exactly what you would imagine from the movies, right down to the guys with Uzis, dark suits, and sunglasses guarding the front door. Clayne's contact had clearly never had an original thought in his life, but that didn't really matter in the cocaine business.

Clayne told me to keep my eyes down when I went in until he said it was okay. He went off to talk with his connection. I was too scared to look up or say a word. We eventually wound up in a huge room with more men, more guns, and the biggest pile of cocaine I ever saw. But it was clear that Clayne's friend was furious with him for having brought someone he didn't know into his house. And it didn't help that I refused to sample the cocaine, having never tried it before and figuring this was not the best time to start.

The repercussions of that reckless visit hit me just a few weeks after Clayne's funeral. Apparently, the dealers worried that I would somehow connect my brother's death with their business—and that I would tell the police and bring them to the man's house. That would obviously have been a problem for them. So now, I was the problem.

I think I had driven to Smith's, the grocery store where I'd shopped so often for food with my moms when I was a child. I'm pretty sure that it was there, in Smith's parking lot, that the three guys were waiting for me when I got back to my car. Again, a lot of this time is really confused. But I know that they pulled up next to me in a Lincoln Continental.

Before I even knew what was happening, they pushed me into the backseat, blindfolded me, and tied my hands behind my back. I was sure I was going to be killed. I knew immediately who they were, but I have no idea where they took me because I was blindfolded. They drove around for a while and then pushed me out of the car. They told me that Clayne had worked for them and wouldn't want me to say anything about it.

"If you want problems, just go to the police and start shit up," one said. "But I would suggest you don't. If you want a quiet, happy life, just forget it."

And then they started beating on me, punching and kicking and hitting from all directions while I was helpless on the ground. When they were done, they drove me back to my car and said "See ya." I straggled back to my parents' house, horrifying my mother with a black eye and numerous bruises. She had begun to dread seeing or hearing from us boys, fearing for our lives. The next shock my family would suffer, however, did not involve the younger generation—but the older one.

TWENTY

A Prophet Dies

I didn't think I would ever find myself back at the enormous Leroy S. Johnson Meeting Hall in Colorado City. I had been there numerous times for priesthood meetings, church services, and Saturday work projects when I'd lived in Short Creek. Now the unadorned building looked especially stark against the red rock cliffs. With Warren's security guards everywhere, I wasn't sure I was going to be allowed to walk through its plain wooden doors one last time.

Prophet Rulon Jeffs had died on September 8, 2002. He was ninety-three. Like his predecessor Uncle Roy, Grandfather had promised to hand the priesthood keys back to Jesus at the second coming—and he'd said he'd live another 350 years into the new millennium. But he had turned out to be mortal, too. I could see that almost everyone in the FLDS had turned out for the funeral. Hundreds of cars and people surrounded us. Almost a week had passed since Rulon had died, and it was now time to bury the prophet.

Warren's sentries stopped us as we approached the main entrance.

These were young men whom he saw as especially loyal and strong, whom he'd chosen as his personal bodyguards. Most of them were my cousins whom I knew well from school and the compound. They scrambled to the entrance as soon as they saw us coming.

Mom, Dad, and almost all of my sisters and brothers who were no longer in the church had driven down in their own cars. I'd traveled with Nathan. But his mom, Felicia, had stayed in Salt Lake, along with my sister Patricia and her youngest children. The rest of us gathered in the parking lot beforehand, trying to prepare ourselves for the hostility that we knew we would face. Dad had called Warren, who had reluctantly agreed to let us view the body—but he said that only Dad could stay for the funeral itself.

Apostates were the last people the church wanted to attend a prophet's funeral, even if they were the prophet's own family. We were even less tolerable than the media, who, while not giving the church the kind of 24/7 attention it would get after I filed my lawsuit, were still drawn to this peculiar spectacle. Even the *New York Times* sent a reporter.

Dad was out front now, talking to the officious young men with earpieces. The faithful church members either stared daggers at us or refused to make eye contact—even my close cousins and people who had been friends for most of my life. I looked around for a sympathetic face, hoping especially to catch sight of Lisa. But I didn't see her and no one else would say a word or even return a slight smile of recognition. I could feel their barely disguised rage.

I hadn't yet removed the backward baseball cap or earrings I was wearing along with my dress shirt and pants. Dad told me to take off the hat, but I wouldn't—not until I got into the building. I wasn't going to defer to these people! I had no respect left for them. Dad was wearing a black suit and my sisters and Mom were dressed in pastel skirts or dresses. The church women wore the same colors, but my sisters' hair wasn't in the front "wave" that FLDS women now wore, virtually without exception.

As Warren had exerted more and more control over the church, the members' wardrobes and hairstyles became increasingly similar. When I was growing up, there was at least some variety in our hairstyles and clothing. But now, it was as though they were converging on a single uniform for each gender. No one wanted to stand out or draw attention to themselves in any way.

Even those who didn't know us—a tiny minority of the five thousand people attending—could see that we stood out. Some seemed to be whispering about Rulon's apostate son and his family, but they continued to refuse to say anything to our faces. My heart pounded as I felt the fear and hatred being directed at us.

These people had been my schoolmates, my cousins, uncles, aunts, and grandmothers—and my first girlfriend. We'd met earlier with my brother Aaron and sister Sara, who still live in Colorado City. We didn't want to get them in trouble by making them acknowledge us publicly. It had come to that.

Now no one would even say a kind word to a man who had lost his father or to his wife and children, who had once been a near-daily part of the prophet's life. I tried to say hi to the father of one of my closest friends from the creek, but he didn't respond. The church members around us looked like zombies. I couldn't see any individuality left, even among the kids.

The security people looked worried even as they tried to intimidate us. Their plan was to let us view the body and move us out as quickly as possible, to avoid a protracted and potentially violent scene. With at least a half dozen guards around us, we were escorted rapidly into the main meeting hall, where Rulon's coffin was laid out on the stage.

We walked behind my father and mother. All of us held our heads high in defiance. Dad moved with quiet dignity, not letting Warren's stripling troops rush him. I stopped trying to get people to acknowledge me and now stared back openly at those who tried to shame me with their looks. I didn't give a shit what they thought. I had every right to be there. But I was on edge because I knew I would soon see Warren. I had steeled myself for that, because it was important for me to do this for my father.

When Dad had learned of Rulon's death from friends in the church who secretly stayed in touch, he had called me. He said I didn't have to go to the funeral if I didn't want to, but he needed to go out of respect for his father. I said I would go. I wanted to be there for him. He seemed proud.

As the guards moved us past the crowds toward the front of the meeting hall, I saw Warren standing near the coffin. To me, he didn't look like he was in mourning for his father. In fact, he seemed eager for the funeral to be done with. I realized that I would have to pass him directly as I neared Grandfather's body. Dad walked past first, not giving Warren even a glance. But I decided I didn't want to do that.

For Clayne's sake—and though I didn't fully realize it at the time, my own too—I wanted to make him face me, to show him that he didn't destroy all of us. I wanted him to feel powerless, for once. I knew I couldn't take physical revenge. This wasn't the place. But that didn't mean I couldn't send a message.

When I approached, I stared him right in the eyes. I even shook his hand. I held steady eye contact all the while. In those few seconds, I saw his pupils widen in fear and his face go pale and gray as he saw that I knew he was a fraud and a pedophile—and that I wasn't a scared little boy anymore. He turned away like the coward that he is, but I felt like I'd put him on notice. And boy, did that feel good.

––––––

I moved on to view the body, but I didn't really feel anything. I had never been close with Grandfather. I'd only really seen him in his ceremonial roles, taking our tithing or preaching. But Dad was devastated. He wasn't crying, but I could see it in his face. He hadn't once spoken with his father since the day Rulon had forced him to choose between our family and the church. I think in the back of his mind he always hoped for some reconciliation. Now there would be none. Seeing Dad's grief made me somber.

I wondered what would happen to the church now—or really, what Warren would do now that he finally officially had the power he'd lusted after for so long. What would he do if someone tried to challenge his right to the actual title? After all, the prophet's position had rarely passed from father to son in the church's history. What if someone else—like one of the powerful Barlow men—stood up?

The only emotion I could see on most people's faces was confusion. Having been out of the church for a while, I started to wonder how they could keep their faith despite prophecies that always seemed to fail. LeRoy Johnson hadn't lived till the second coming; Rulon Jeffs didn't die in 2350. Nor did he have his body "renewed." Warren had repeatedly claimed that this would happen, even writing a song about it. He said that Grandfather's strokes had been God's way of letting him rest, but that he would soon be restored to youthful vigor so that he could lead and impregnate his then more than sixty wives, many of whom were very young. But there he was, frail and gray in his coffin.

No fewer than three times, Rulon had set dates when he claimed the righteous people of our church would be "lifted up" into heaven, while the sinners would be annihilated in the apocalypse. Afterward, he predicted, the chosen ones would return, to rule the world and worship in peace. Each of the appointed days for this "elevation" were filled with celebration, as the people gathered in an open field near the Colorado City graveyard on a specially built platform called the "launching pad."

But the groceries everyone had brought as instructed to tide them over for the journey through space did not accompany them up to heaven. Nothing happened, and when midnight neared each time and God hadn't elevated them, Rulon simply declared that the people had not been faithful enough and needed more time to repent before He would fulfill the prophecy.

The last of these falsely predicted apocalypses was June 12, 1999. That day was special because it would have been Uncle Roy's one hundred eleventh birthday. Before proceeding to the launching pad, everyone had gathered in a prayer circle at 6 a.m. in the parking lot of the meeting hall, singing hymns. But when the day came to a close, once again Rulon said the people were not pure or ready enough for elevation.

Undeterred by his record of failed predictions, my grandfather made another bold prophecy. He proclaimed in December 1999 that the 2002 Salt Lake Olympics would bring a terrorist attack and widespread destruction. To avoid this, he ordered his Salt Lake followers to move to Colorado City. He and Warren led them, having built a huge house for themselves in Short Creek, the one that took up an entire city block.

Most members complied and sold their property—some taking a large financial hit, which was no problem because the world was ending anyway. Their creditors were not as credulous. I even heard that some people in Short Creek celebrated when they learned about the fall of the twin towers on 9/11, seeing the attacks as the fulfillment of this prophecy.

Although I'd believed in my religion as a small child, it now seemed to me to be completely absurd. "How could these people still take this all so seriously?" I wondered, watching my family file past Grandfather's coffin. It was now obvious to me that the prophet was just an old man, nothing more. But of course, I also knew exactly why the church members still believed.

When everyone else around you believes, when every single person you know acts as though something is true, when you have been taught it every day since infancy, it really is hard to stand up. Being instructed day in and day out to value obedience, to see faith as higher than reason, and to discard independent thinking as a sign of possession by the devil makes it even more difficult. And growing up in a huge family where you are just one of many and have to go along just to get along every day makes you more susceptible yet.

I was glad we wouldn't be staying for Warren's eulogy. I wanted to get out of that creepy world and back to the real one as quickly as possible. As much as they worried about being corrupted by our "evil," I found myself concerned about their influence on my family. I was hugely relieved to be back in the car with Nathan and driving as fast and as far away from there as we could.

Although I didn't know it for sure, by the time of Grandfather's funeral, Warren had already completed his official takeover. Not long before he died, Grandfather seemed to recognize that he'd been usurped. "I want my job back!" he demanded in a moment of lucidity. Of course, Warren smoothly assured him that he'd never lost it.

And then, Rulon passed. I have heard rumors that he was smothered in his bed by Warren, who had grown tired of waiting to take full command. Supposedly, that story came from one of Rulon's wives, who witnessed the killing, but there is no way to know if it is true.

Other accounts say that Warren and Fred Jessop—the ninety-something bishop of Short Creek and one of Rulon's closest advisers—were gathered respectfully near Grandfather's bedside when he left this world. Reportedly, Warren said to Fred that he supposed the mantle of prophecy now belonged to the older man, but Fred declined and said that it was rightly Warren's. The transition had been completed before

Rulon's body was even cold. If this is what happened, Fred would rapidly regret his choice.

Just a few days after Rulon's death, Warren preached at the morning meeting of his new school in Short Creek that it was "a wonderful occasion" and that the students present were all "privileged to meet at priesthood schools.

"We were sent to this earth to learn who God is and to become like Him. Prophets have been sent who, through obedience, became like God . . . There is a pruning going on. We want to be perfected and step up, not cast off . . . I say this rejoicing in God and the Godhead."[1]

But to many, it seemed like he was rejoicing in more earthly pleasures. In fact, the day after his father's death he had assembled the community in the meeting hall to officially announce the prophet's passage and the circumstances around it. Then, to the great shock of all who were listening, Warren proclaimed, "I won't say much but I will say this: 'Hands off my father's wives.' " To Grandfather's widows he then said, "You women will live as if father is still alive in the next room."[2]

Within a week, he had received revelations about which of his father's widows were "worthy" of him—and soon secretly married them. According to one account, only two of the "chosen" turned him down.[3] Needless to say, the women he selected were not among the older ones who had raised, and in one case, borne him.

Warren's own mother, Merilyn, had been Rulon's fourth wife. She had schemed for so long to bring Warren to power that I would love to know what she was thinking when she heard that her son's first priority upon becoming prophet was to ensure that he got his pick of her youngest and prettiest sister-wives. In the church it was traditional for the next prophet to take care of the wives of the prior patriarch, but it wasn't traditional for the successor to be his son. Uncle Roy had preached that sons should not take their father's wives if this happened. So Warren's actions were stunning to many church members. Merilyn remains involved with the church, however, so there is no way to find out what she thought of it.

I was proud of myself for having been able to support my dad, and for not shying away when I saw Warren. But while that felt good person-

ally, I soon began to think it wasn't enough. Why should a criminal like
him go free—and even worse, run a powerful church ten thousand
strong, with unlimited access to children?

In the years leading up to Grandfather's death, Warren had been
named trustee of the United Effort Plan. This organization owned virtually all of the property in Colorado City and Hildale. Early in Mormon history, Joseph Smith had decided that communal ownership of
property would end poverty and allow all church members to flourish.
But in reality, the arrangement gave the church leadership tremendous
power. If a member displeased the top men, he could lose his home and
all the equity that had gone into it. And if he also worked for a church-
run business, as many in Short Creek now did, he could find himself
facing not only homelessness but also unemployment.

Uncle Roy had rarely used the prophet's power to "reassign" men's
wives and children if he thought they were failing to live up to their role
in the priesthood. But—as my father and my family had learned
painfully—Rulon had taken this power for himself. Since he'd won the
fight over one-man rule with the earlier leadership and assumed final
veto over all important decisions in the FLDS, the prophet now had
unchecked power to split families, take homes, and assign or reassign
jobs. And after Warren had become trustee, he'd convinced more and
more members to turn over their businesses and their retirement sav-
ings to the church, increasing its wealth. The trust's value has been esti-
mated at $110 million.[4]

The man who was, to my mind, responsible for the death of my
brother Clayne should not have that kind of power. Not only was it infuriating and unjust—it was dangerous. I had seen my former friends
and family members at the funeral. They weren't themselves. They
were completely at his mercy, which was nonexistent. I wanted to do
something about it. But I had no idea what—and my own ability to handle even the most ordinary tasks in life was about to be seriously chal-
lenged.

TWENTY-ONE

Lost and Found

The credit card made a rhythmic, clicking sound as Big D chopped up the pearly, shalelike rocks of cocaine on a mirror. He'd bought an eighth of an ounce, and now I was at his apartment, about to try coke for the first time. My older brothers had been pretty rigorous about keeping hard drugs away from me when I was younger, but after Clayne died, everything started falling apart. Between his death and Rulon's death, late 2002 and early 2003 were a blur of mourning, obligation, and escape.

Dave was the closest of my brothers to Clayne and the loss had hit him really hard. In fact, the only time we ever talked about it was when we did coke. He rolled up a twenty-dollar bill, did a line, and passed the mirror to me. It felt really strange to sniff something into my nose deliberately—and I was quite scared of this drug, with its wicked reputation. But I figured, what the fuck. Dave had told me it was pretty mellow stuff and I was curious.

It wasn't at all what I expected. I'd spent a lot of weekends at clubs, taking Ecstasy and losing myself in the music. Other times, I'd eaten mushrooms, tripping out with my friends, looking at the stars. Clayne, in fact, had had to talk me down from my worst trip. I had called him at three in the morning one weekend and he'd left his wife and kids to spend four or five hours with me to chill me out. I believed that I had gone insane. I couldn't tell what was real and what wasn't. I was afraid I would never come down. Clayne sat there with me all night, telling me it would be all right, keeping me company till I could sleep.

But coke was nothing like shrooms. I guess I thought it would be more overpowering, less functional, further away from a sense of reality. When I snorted it, I just felt wonderful, like I could control everything and that all good things were possible. I didn't feel out of it—I felt on top of it. Dave was able to confide in me how terribly he missed Clayne and to talk about the problems in his marriage. I felt safe enough to talk to him about my sadness over Clayne's death and the chaos of my life at that time. It was like that feeling I sometimes got when I blanked out to avoid my past.

But when Clayne died, the small amount of order I'd managed to bring into my life began to slip away. I had finished high school via home study and I was pretty much always working, but my living situation was chronically unstable. I moved from place to place and job to job, sometimes living with my brothers, other times renting rooms in friends' basements, never staying anywhere for much more than a year. I had no goals and no real direction.

I had also tried an engagement that ended in disaster. I'd met a Mormon girl who had a close, loving family. I'd spent lots of time with her and with them, even working for her father for a while. We were involved for about a year and a half when I proposed and she accepted. I thought I was ready to settle down and that getting married might give my life more structure.

Then her parents began pressuring me to get baptized in the LDS. The LDS church does not view the FLDS as a "true" church—so I would have to start from scratch. She pushed me too because she wanted to get married in the temple. I didn't really believe in the religion, but I figured I'd do it for her. So I agreed to convert, and for weeks I met with two Mormon missionaries who were going to perform my baptism. Because of my endless education in scripture at Alta, I easily impressed them with my knowledge of the religion: I probably could have converted them had I been so inclined.

However, when Clayne died, I couldn't manage the relationship anymore. I wasn't able to be there for her. We had a messy breakup, which left me feeling betrayed and hurt.

Between my broken engagement and losing Clayne and being beaten by those drug dealers, I was spinning out of control. I worked various construction jobs and smoked about an eighth of an ounce of pot every day. Prior to Clayne's death, I'd tried to avoid taking drugs at work, and right after he died, I didn't do any drugs at all. But now I was smoking every day again and getting drunk a lot. And I was starting to get involved with coke.

I landed in my friend Chandler's basement. And there my life got much, much better—before it took its most serious turn for the worse.

Chandler's girlfriend had a friend she thought would be perfect for me. She invited her to one of our parties to set us up. Chandler's house was right near our old compound. It was really his mom's place—a large, ostentatious, and expensive home.

Chandler's mother and siblings lived upstairs. We had the basement all to ourselves. It had a big rec room with a large-screen TV, pool table, great speakers, a refrigerator for beer—pretty much everything a young man could want. I rented one of the large bedrooms down there.

Following the end of my engagement, I had become quite suspicious of women. Dave had also suffered a serious betrayal—that was one of the things we talked about when we did coke. I'd had my heart broken. I was trying to protect myself. I had never paid attention to those rap lyrics about "bitches and hos" because I'd been raised to treat women with respect, but I had a wall up now.

So, my room was set up like a bachelor pad. There was a Bud Light poster, a black light pointed at a psychedelic mushroom poster, and a safe with a bumper sticker on it. It said "I ♥ Mormon pussy." One of my friends had put the same sticker on the back of his car, but I wasn't crazy enough to drive around like that in Salt Lake City! I had a comforter and sheet set in a black-and-yellow leopard print. It was your basic looking-for-a-good-time, lost boy stoner room.

Except for one thing: everything was in place, dusted, neat, and clean. Many lost boys lived in party central, where cleanliness and order were not exactly a priority. Not my room. The bed was made. The black light was at the right angle to spotlight the poster. The knickknacks on my dresser—my collection of pipes, knives, and lighters, along with some glass figurines—were spaced just so. When Jody first saw the place, she later joked that she had thought I couldn't be straight. But then she saw the bumper sticker and, well, me.

We fell in love pretty much at first sight. My fears about being betrayed just left: I knew she was different. Jody has long, thick black hair and striking blue-green eyes that shift toward blue when she's happy and green when she's low. She saw me in my hoodie sweater, baggy pants, and blond-tipped hair and thought I was cute. I thought she was gorgeous and we started cuddling almost right away. She was seventeen and I was twenty.

She was curious about my background and asked me many questions, but I never felt she was judging me. I could relax around her in a way that I really couldn't with other people.

After we met, we rarely spent a night apart. But within a few months, I had to move again. I had left $300 to pay my rent on Chandler's mom's dresser, like I usually did. Someone must have stolen it. Whatever happened, Chandler's mom claimed I didn't pay it. I didn't have enough money to pay my rent twice, so I moved out. An older woman I knew— not the one I'd lived with before—was renovating her house at that time and needed some work done. So I moved in with her, bartering the work for the room. Officially, Jody still lived with her parents, but she spent most nights there with me.

Meeting Jody may have saved my life. Someone that she was very close to had had a cocaine problem, so I knew I couldn't do that around her. With Dave, I had been doing it on weekends. Even though I hated the crash and the "speeded-up" feeling it sometimes gave me, I watched many people go on doing it despite that. I feel like I dodged a bullet: I'm really glad my brothers had protected me from it when I was younger, because I think if I had started it then, I wouldn't have been able to stop.

Also, being part of a couple, I spent a lot less time in clubs, where I'd done some of my heaviest partying. Being with Jody meant that I had less time to get drunk or hang out with Dave, who was using prescription pain medications as well as cocaine—though I still smoked weed every day.

Jody was a calming presence. She was an anchor for me, creating real stability for the first time since I had left the church. I really wanted a normal life. Unfortunately, the turmoil that Clayne's death had stirred up in me was still there. The weed was one symptom. My fury that Warren was now running the show—which came out against all kinds of inappropriate targets, including, unfortunately, Jody herself at times—was another.

I loved Clayne and I missed him, but I wasn't sure why I felt so personally affronted by what had happened to him. It seemed like there was something missing, something I'd caught glimpses of but couldn't quite grasp. I was still on edge a lot of the time, and alternatively in a fog where I felt I couldn't quite reach people. Jody sometimes complained that I wasn't paying attention, that I wasn't really there. I knew it was true, but I didn't know why or what I could do about it. And then, after all that time, all that running, things started to come back to me.

TWENTY-TWO

Nightmares and Revelations

I woke up thrashing in bed and covered with sweat. Since I'd been kidnapped by the drug dealers I'd had occasional nightmares. I thought at first that they were related to the fear I'd had when blindfolded or to seeing Clayne's broken body. But I couldn't understand why that would make me dream about elementary school. Or why my dreams of being back at Alta Academy so completely terrorized me.

My heart was racing and blood pumping furiously as I tried to figure out where I was and what had happened. The fear was sometimes so intense that I felt unable to breathe and in danger of losing control of myself entirely. I couldn't shake it off. When I had these dreams, they colored my mood for hours. The taste of fear and a sense of panic raced through my body, keeping me constantly on edge. My heart just wouldn't slow down and my stomach burned.

As I came to that night, I saw that Jody was there and she was trying to help me. I don't know why these dreams began to afflict me so frequently when I was with Jody, but I think it may have been that I felt safe enough with her to finally recall my terrible memories.

At first, however, I was afraid to tell her what was really scaring me. I described my dream to her, but I didn't say anything more than that. The dream was just a set of images connected only by fear. It didn't make much sense to me; I'm sure it made even less to her. She hugged me, holding me close, telling me everything was going to be okay. She kept saying that it was only a dream. But as the nightmares recurred, I began to realize that that might not be true.

In the first dream that I was able to articulate, I immediately recognized that I was at Alta. The hallways seemed huge, so I felt like I must've been a very little kid. And then I saw Warren's hand, and his tall gawky frame looming over me, taking me somewhere. We were walking down the long, dark, wood-paneled halls in the basement; he was pulling me behind him.

At first, that's when I'd wake up, just going down the hall. But I'd be drenched in sweat, screaming and feeling as though I was paralyzed. It was one of the most frightening experiences you can imagine, like being buried alive and conscious but unable to do anything about it.

As I began to have the nightmares more often, the intensity of these experiences became overwhelming. The nights that I had the dreams, I was exhausted the whole next day. I had no idea what was going on. Worse, the dreams became more frequent.

When I slept, my mind flooded with images of Warren, the sense of being in a classroom with my kindergarten and toddler cousins, glimpses of the hallways at Alta. Then it would all go red in an overpowering explosion of terror and pain.

These images were repetitive, and sometimes I wasn't even sure if I was awake or asleep. They were much more vivid than other dreams—and not like regular memories, either. It was as though I was reliving something. Not as an adult thinking back to childhood: I was there as a child, with all the pain and fear and inarticulate terror that I had blocked out at the time.

I began to dread going to sleep. By this point, I already smoked way too much pot—but now I even began smoking at work. I started taking over-the-counter sleeping pills, but they didn't help much.

Soon Jody told me that I was talking—actually screaming—in my sleep. Most of it other than "No" and "Please, stop" was incomprehensible, but now she too felt that it seemed like I was reliving something awful. She'd wake me up and try to calm me down. But that was difficult. It was often hours before I could relax.

I didn't know what to do. I tried ignoring the dreams, hoping they'd go away. It took everything I had to make myself drag my ass to work, pushing through each day, like a robot. I did my job and paid my bills and didn't care about anything or anyone else. If Jody had a problem, I'd tell her to suck it up. I couldn't listen to anyone or be there for them.

Like my dad, I began to have outbursts of sheer rage. I would get home from work and if any little thing was out of place in our apartment, I'd completely lose it. I could see in her eyes that I was scaring Jody, but I just found any kind of sloppiness infuriating. I shouted at her. Part of me realized that I was blowing up over nothing, but I couldn't seem to stop. At the moment I exploded, I felt as though I could have no peace if the apartment was not perfectly ordered. It felt like she was trying to destroy me by failing to keep my home the way I wanted it, like it was some kind of profound insult and disrespect.

I knew that I was being irrational, even cruel. I knew how much I had suffered from my dad's temper. But I just couldn't stand not being in total control of my environment. I had lost control of so much else that having everything in its place seemed like the most important thing in the world at those times.

Other shards of memory started slicing up my dreams. I began to see the pale blue tiles in the bathroom and the tub. I would hear the bathroom door slamming and locking. I would see the classroom and the other kids, before Warren took me out. Later, I started to hear Warren's oily voice, and see the icy blank look in his eyes. I'd see him hovering over me. And over and over, I would feel the overwhelming pain and the total powerlessness I felt when I was raped.

At one point, I saw images of being inside one of those secret passages and being pulled along by Warren. I saw the cold looks on his brothers' faces as they deferred to him and failed to help me. I saw the grotesque expression of triumph and hatred Warren had when he was finished. I felt his hand silencing my screams. After keeping it locked up for so long, my mind hit me with everything, night after night after night.

I had to face it: these were memories, not my imagination and not ordinary dreams. They were too vivid, too real. That kid in the bathtub being raped was me; there was no way around that reality.

And as the night terrors continued, I realized I had to tell Jody what I now knew to be true. I was afraid. I didn't want her to think less of me. I was embarrassed and ashamed. I thought that she might think I wasn't really a man—that this had somehow taken that away from me. I felt filthy and repellent and disgusting. It seemed like the world was closing in on me, collapsing all around me. I couldn't even trust my own mind.

One morning, I was lying in bed with her and I began to feel sick. My heart felt like it was going to jump out of my chest. "I don't feel good," was all I managed to say.

"What's wrong?" she asked, seeing that I had gone white.

"Something really bad happened to me," I stammered. "My mind is not okay."

"What do you mean?"

"Something really bad is inside of me. I'm dirty." I knew I wasn't making any sense, but I wasn't yet able to express what was happening. Just saying that much made the panic worse. I felt like I was suffocating, that I couldn't get enough air into my lungs.

"I'm going to die," I gasped. "I can't breathe. I can't do this."

Tears began streaming down my face and Jody didn't know what to do. By now, she was crying too, so she decided to call my mom and took me over there. Mom hugged me and put a cold washcloth on my face, telling me it was okay and that I was having a panic attack.

After a horrifying hour or so, it passed and I was able to forget about it and go to work the next day. Then, a few nights later when I was trying to fall asleep, I started feeling the same way again. Jody had her back to me. I sat up and said, "I have to tell you something. I'm starting to remember." She turned toward me and I said, "I don't want you to think badly of me. It's starting to come back." I began to weep silently.

She said, "I won't, I promise. What happened?"

I just said it. "I was raped when I was really young."

I was bawling now. I had finally put it into words. I had said it out loud. I was so scared that she would abandon me. But she just accepted it and asked me to tell her more. She held me and I cried and cried and cried. I gave her some more details, watching her face closely as I told her. To my great relief, all I saw was compassion. It felt like a huge weight had been lifted off my chest. Her acceptance meant the world to me.

I still didn't know what I was supposed to do. I wondered if I was always going to be like this and the thought terrified me. I didn't know if I could take much more. I was barely hanging on at work and at home. The nightmares kept coming. I wasn't really sleeping and I felt like I was going to go crazy.

One time, I woke Jody by growling in my sleep, making a noise that seemed more animal than human. She couldn't wake me up. Terrified, she shook me, moving my arms, eventually shouting. I was completely unresponsive. My eyes were rolled back in my head and finally she slapped me across the face. I woke and couldn't speak. I could describe some of the images later—like the hallway or Warren's face—but mostly, my dreams were storms of pure emotion, none of it good.

I felt trapped. I didn't want to tell my parents because I knew how hurt they'd be to know that Warren had molested not one but two of their boys. But soon I realized that I had no choice. If I didn't tell them and didn't try to get some kind of help, what had happened to Clayne could happen to me. I began to see myself as a lifelong druggie, picturing myself dead of an overdose. I couldn't see any other future. I didn't want to kill myself. I had seen how Clayne's suicide had hurt so many people.

I had sworn I would never use heroin, after watching how it had taken over Clayne's life. I knew it must have helped him cope with these feelings, though, and I felt like I would not be able to resist it if my life continued this way.

Now Jody began to plead with me to get help. "You need to tell your parents," she'd say. "You need to get a hold on this. If you don't, it's going to haunt you forever and it's not worth it." I knew she was right. Somehow, it was still hard to take that first step.

Fortunately, not long after this, Jody and I had dinner with Mom and Dad and one of my sisters and her husband. We went early, and I used the opportunity to take Mom aside and tell her. She started bawling and Jody and I had to calm her down. I had been afraid of that—I knew it wasn't her fault, but I knew she would think it was. She felt so bad that she hadn't been able to protect us.

She hugged me and told me she loved me and how sorry she was about what had happened. By the time everyone else arrived, she had pulled herself together and we had an ordinary family dinner. All of us had had a lot of practice at pretending everything was okay when it wasn't. I knew she would discuss it with Dad, and after that, I was able to talk with him about it.

Now I really felt I had to do something to stop Warren. My anger over what had happened to me and over Clayne's death continued to grow. There had to be something I could do. I didn't know anything about the law or the legal system, but surely there must be some way to hold him accountable? No one should be able to get away with what he had done. Being a self-proclaimed prophet didn't make him above the law. This was America, not Afghanistan. Finally, I realized that there was someone I knew who might know, someone who might just be willing and able to help.

PART FOUR

FIGHTING BACK

TWENTY-THREE

Seeking Justice

Dr. Dan Fischer—a friend of my dad's—had become a wealthy and powerful man. He'd grown up in the FLDS. Like my dad, he'd had three wives, two of whom were sisters. When Dr. Fischer was in high school, Uncle Roy had decided that the church needed a dentist. Dan had gone to the prophet's office, expecting to be assigned a construction job as a work mission, but he was told instead that he was to go to college and then on to dental school.

Dr. Fischer is not sure why he was selected, but he was a bright, capable student and figures his good grades must've helped. He had longed for more education, so the assignment delighted him. A dutiful church member, he completed his schooling and became our community dentist, treating most of the children and adults in the FLDS. He treated the kids in our family when we were little.

When he couldn't find dental products to meet his needs, he began designing what he wanted himself and making it in his garage. He'd prospered as a result. In the 1970s and '80s he invented numerous materials like teeth whiteners and dental implements, patenting them and becoming a multimillionaire. Chances are, if you've had serious dental work, you've had some of his products in your mouth.

But as Warren began to take over and started enforcing all his rules and splitting up families, Dr. Fischer lost faith in the FLDS. He left the church—but our families had stayed in touch. Over the years, he helped lots of lost boys get on their feet, often by hiring them himself. I had worked for him twice—once when I'd first left the church as a teenager, doing construction, and now as a machinist.

I went to see him, deciding that if anyone could help find a legal way to hold Warren accountable, it would be Dr. Fischer. I talked to him about what Warren had done to Clayne, and what I now knew he'd done to me as well. I asked for his help. Dan had founded an organization that was becoming more and more involved in the plight of boys who had left the FLDS.

He'd originally organized the nonprofit Diversity Foundation (also called Smiles for Diversity) for a somewhat different purpose. Growing up as a "plyg kid," he was sensitive to the plight of stigmatized minorities and knew what it was like to be ostracized for being different. He also became horrified by the racist teachings that the FLDS had espoused.

In the late '90s a series of events crystallized his sense that there was a need for a local organization to promote tolerance. Utah is still a very white, overwhelmingly Mormon state. In fact, this whole part of the West has had a serious problem with hate crimes. In 1998, near Laramie, Wyoming, twenty-one-year-old Matthew Shepard was beaten to death because he was gay.

That same year, James Byrd, an African American, was killed in Jasper, Texas, when racists dragged him behind their truck. And, in April 1999, the Columbine High School shootings left thirteen dead in an act of rage and hatred that coincided with Hitler's birthday. So Diversity's initial mission was to fight hate crimes by using comics to teach young children about cultural differences and to value diversity rather than fear it.

As Warren tightened his grip over the FLDS—and took more and more young wives for himself and other high-ranking church members—hundreds of young men began to leave or be forced out of the group. Clayne's example was one of the more tragic, but all of my older brothers and I had suffered as we left.

We'd been luckier than some because our mom had always maintained contact, and Dad had even allowed Dave and Clayne to come back home at low points in their addictions. Still, all the boys who left in their teens struggled with lack of education, loss of family and community, and loss of financial support from their parents. Usually, they became involved with alcohol and other drugs, too. Of the hundreds of boys seen by Diversity, there were very few who didn't have at least some period of heavy substance abuse.

With most people unaware of the problem—and even fewer with the means to do anything to help—Dan and Diversity had been drafted to fill the void. I thought that if we could somehow bring Warren to justice, we might be able to help all the lost boys and prevent more families from being destroyed.

Dr. Fischer listened to me and told me he thought the idea was a good one. By 2004, he had become even more worried about the situation. In 1999, Warren had split up Dan's father's family, leaving one of his youngest sisters crying, "If Father does really well, can he please be our father again?" Warren had replied coldly, "There's not enough time."

Since I'd left, the talk of the apocalypse and the frenzied attempt at "perfection" to cause God to lift the people up to heaven had only intensified. Warren was also arranging the marriages of younger and younger girls. When Dad had married Vera, it was relatively rare for teenage girls to be married at sixteen—and that had happened at her own instigation. Now, however, Warren was marrying fourteen-, thirteen-, even twelve-year-olds—and it didn't have anything to do with the girls' wishes.

Some of these girls had started to run away. Some women who had lived polygamy were helping them and also organizing efforts to get the police to enforce the bigamy laws and those against underage marriage. But at this time, none of the girls who were victimized by forced underage marriages had come forward to seek justice. They were terrified that their parents or other family members would be punished if they went to the authorities. They didn't want their families to be split up or to lose their homes. Many of the girls were just as lost as we boys were. They feared that the Gentile world was as corrupt as they'd been taught.

Given the way the town authorities operated in Colorado City and Hildale, this was a belief that had some basis in their own experience. As I'd discovered during my time there, the Short Creek cops didn't primarily enforce state or federal law—they served as the prophet's private force. All of the local police and ambulance corps were members of the FLDS, and they believed that what they saw as God's law took priority over the laws of men.

If a woman complained about domestic violence or child abuse, nothing was done other than reporting the complaint to the prophet. If teenagers stayed out after Warren's curfew, they'd be arrested and brought home—but no charges would be filed. They couldn't be: they weren't actually doing anything illegal. If a woman wanted an ambulance to take her to the hospital, it wouldn't leave the twin towns until her husband's permission had been granted.

Coming from that world, it was hard to believe in justice, and when the community you've been taught has all the answers turns on you, it's hard to believe that outsiders whom you have been taught are evil will do any better. Even if you no longer believe that Gentiles are devils, it's still difficult to avoid acting as if they are. In fact, I think the hardest part of leaving the FLDS is constantly fighting these battles in your own mind.

I knew that taking Warren on was a formidable task. It would be like trying to bring down a king who ran his own country with his own army. But my anger over how Clayne and I—and the rest of my family—had been treated wouldn't let me rest. I told Dr. Fischer that I was willing to do anything to help. If it took going public about the abuse I had suffered, I would do that.

He said he'd find—and pay—an attorney, if there was a way to use the legal system in this fight. During this process, he also said that he thought I needed professional counseling—to deal with the nightmares and the memories and with the attacks from the church that going to court would invariably involve. He recommended Dr. Larry Bill, who had treated other former FLDS members. I agreed to go. But first, he had to find a lawyer who would take the case.

TWENTY-FOUR

Legal Action

The lobby was hushed, with posh carpeting, marble floors, and high ceilings. I don't think I'd ever been in such a nice hotel before. I was already nervous, but feeling so out of place didn't help. The woman I had come to see was even more intimidating: Joanne Suder was an East Coast lawyer with a strong New York accent and many multimillion-dollar judgments under her belt. Dad, Don, and I had flown out to Orange County to meet with her and see if she thought I had a case. I am not sure why we met in California, but it did give us a chance to relax on the beach afterward.

And I would need that. I was about to tell a woman who I didn't really know my most dreadful secrets. I had only started to accept what had happened to me. I hadn't yet begun therapy. What would she ask me? How would I feel if she didn't believe me?

I tried to look around me to distract myself. It seemed like everyone was wearing a suit or at least very expensive clothes. They all seemed to belong there and know what they were doing. Joanne fit in, too: she looked every bit like the high-powered attorney she was, wearing a crisp suit and small glasses. I felt awkward in my jeans and T-shirt.

Joanne first told me about herself and her work. She had filed over $350 million in lawsuits against the Catholic Church for sexual abuse and had won many millions in settlements for her clients. She had been among the first to take on abuse cases against priests, and was the force behind these suits against the archdiocese of Baltimore.

I didn't know much about Catholics or their church, but I did know it was a huge religion and that the church was wealthy and powerful. Joanne certainly had the qualifications needed to sue Warren and the FLDS.

I think she was trying to impress me, but I was unused to such powerful people, so I actually felt more shy. And as I listened, a wave of shame came over me. I still blamed myself for the abuse. How could I discuss it with a woman I had just met?

I tried to compose myself. I thought about Clayne. This was the only way of getting justice for him. If this could stop Warren from hurting other kids, I had to do it. It wasn't about me. I couldn't chicken out now.

So I took Joanne through my story. I said simply that I had been raped by my uncle, that the same thing had happened to Clayne, and that Clayne had taken his life because of it. I teared up as I told her, but was mostly matter-of-fact. She looked in my eyes and said she believed me and that if this was what had happened, she would take the case. When I heard that, I began to relax.

I told her about our church and about how Warren controlled everything—including the property of everyone who lived in Colorado City and Hildale. I told her how he'd reassigned men's wives to other people and taken their property. She told me that we could probably get millions of dollars. As I walked down the beach later with Dad and Don, looking at the girls in their tiny bikinis, I wondered what it would be like to be as rich as the people who lived here.

———

Back in Salt Lake, I had all kinds of meetings and phone calls about the lawsuit. Joanne had not only taken on my case, she'd also begun work on a case for six other lost boys who were suing the FLDS for having been "systematically" pushed out of the church and their homes. My friend Richie was one of them. Whereas my brothers and I had been among the earliest to leave, the pace picked up dramatically after Rulon died in 2002.

The suit charged Warren and the church with establishing the "secret, cruel, abusive and unlawful practice of reducing the surplus male population by systematically expelling young males from the FLDS communities in which they were raised." This, our lawyers charged, was done to "foster the unlawful and aggressive" practice of polygamy.

According to the lawsuit, the FLDS was "predominantly a criminal enterprise" and the suit was filed to recoup damages "sustained as a result of the [church's] pattern of unlawful activity, fraud, breach of fiduciary duties, breach of assumed duties, alienation of parental affections, inflictions of emotional distress, invasion of privacy and civil conspiracy which arose from the [church's] unconscionable conduct including their practice of expulsion to further the illegal practice of polygamy." In other words, the church was like the mafia and committed numerous crimes in order to sustain its primary illegal business: polygamy. Among these crimes was expelling boys so that the older men had young girls to marry.

Some lost boys were simply excommunicated and expelled by Warren himself—for anything from serious rebellion like Clayne's drug use to something as innocent as watching a movie or playing a video game. In some cases, their parents were instructed to throw "disobedient" boys out themselves—and many did, whether their sins were real or exaggerated. Sometimes, Warren's "sentries" beat up boys before putting them out. As in Clayne's case, many parents felt pressure not to let troubled teens stay at home.

Some mothers actually packed a few clothes for their boys and simply abandoned them on the side of the highway that leads to Colorado City. These parents weren't completely heartless. They were afraid that if they didn't do so, Warren would split the whole family, reassigning wives and children to another man. Many moms cried as they drove their sons out of town. It was a horrible calculus, but many parents felt that losing one family member was better than losing everyone.

The Diversity Foundation estimates that over the years nearly three hundred families have been split this way, affecting thousands of children. Some of the women who have left have said that they began to feel like prostitutes, being moved from one strange man to another.

With the constant preaching about the apocalypse, the threat of family dissolution, and the increasing restrictions on any kind of enjoyable activity, another group of boys simply chose to leave. They saw the writing on the wall: Warren and the church leaders were taking more and more young women for themselves. They were under constant scrutiny for even the tiniest disobedience. Like my dad, these lost boys basically chose to say, "You can't fire me. I quit!"

Our hope with the lost boy lawsuit and my case against Warren was to provide more help for the boys who came after us, offering them guidance and a visible path to a normal life. Unlike most high-school dropouts and other teens with drug and mental health problems, lost boys usually have the added issues of being rejected by their families and community and being expelled from a strict and controlling religion. Most runaways are not worried that their choice to leave home condemns them to eternal damnation. Services aimed at dropouts, addicts, and runaways don't have the capacity to help them with these issues—and we wanted to change that.

It was a gray, rainy day when I visited our old compound with Greg Hoole. It looked pretty much the same as it had when I'd left. But now, my grandfather's house and the Alta Academy building were occupied by a charity that sheltered patients awaiting heart transplants. The patients stayed in the prophet's former home. I felt like I might need a new heart myself after this visit.

Greg was now one of my attorneys: he and his brother Roger had been hired by Dan Fischer as local counsel to work with Joanne Suder. When lawyers are from out of state, they have to hire local counsel if they haven't passed the bar in the state where the case will be tried. Sometimes, even if they are qualified in that state, they do this anyway because local counsel will know the judges and any regional quirks of the legal system better than people from out of town. As Greg and Roger became more involved in the case, they began to have differences of opinion with Joanne. These were ultimately resolved by having her withdraw and Greg and Roger take over.

By the time I met Greg, I'd told my story several times: to Jody, to my parents, and to Joanne. But it never seemed to get much easier and being back at the compound only made it worse.

I took Greg through the now-empty rooms of Alta Academy, describing my school days there and Warren. I showed him the meeting hall where Warren, Rulon, and Uncle Roy had preached. He was surprised by how small the meeting room was—and how haphazardly built. He later joked that the church should have sent someone to architectural school, not just Dan Fischer to dental school. It was true that the FLDS tended to favor function over form.

I also showed him those secret passageways, which were purportedly there in case of a government raid on polygamists but which I think Warren may have used at least once to take me to or from my Sunday school classroom. I showed him the room where I had been baptized and then I took him to that awful bathroom.

I had to fight my desire to flee, but I stayed with it. Although I didn't actually cry, Greg could see how profoundly I'd been harmed by what had happened there. I wasn't able to stay very long, but it was long enough to trigger nightmares. I think it was shortly after this that Jody insisted that I had to start therapy—immediately.

TWENTY-FIVE

Getting Better

Dr. Larry Bill's office was in downtown Salt Lake. I was anxious, but I figured that doing something had to be better than doing nothing. The nightmares had become a near-nightly event and my work and my relationship with Jody were suffering. I was having panic attacks. I knew I had to hold it together if I wanted to work on my lawsuit.

When I walked into his office and shook his hand, the doctor immediately put me at ease. There was something about his deep voice and manner that was warm, calm, and soothing. I could see that he knew how fragile I was and had dealt with similar patients before.

He was an ordinary-looking guy with brown hair, brown eyes, about 5' 10"—nothing stood out about his looks at all. As he explained to me exactly what he would do and why, I began to have the feeling that it was safe to talk about my past. The tension began to drain out of me. Dr. Bill seemed trustworthy, even though I hardly knew him. And the thought crossed my mind that there wasn't any point in seeing someone if I wasn't going to trust him.

He asked me a series of questions about my life, typing my answers into his laptop as he sat with me. His office was filled with books. On one side was the desk where he sat with the computer and on the other was the couch. It was simple and orderly, which helped make me comfortable. He said I could sit or lie down in whatever position was most comfortable and explained that he would use hypnosis to help me tame the memories as much as possible.

He said that they would never go away entirely, but that he was sure that he could help me make them much easier to live with. He told me that I didn't have to live with the rage and the flashbacks and the pain, that he would help me put my memories in their place and keep them from tormenting me every night. The fact that he didn't promise a miracle cure was oddly reassuring. I had had enough of miracles.

The first time, we didn't do much. I lay down on the couch and we tried a brief period of hypnosis to see if I could relax enough to enter that state. Although I wasn't able to stay in it very long or go very deep, I was able to begin the process. It wasn't that different from being in a very calm, focused frame of mind. It wasn't scary or mysterious. In fact, it felt a lot like the Buddhist meditation I'd done a few times with my brother Dave.

Dr. Bill told me to imagine a safe, happy place. I pictured a mountain meadow on a warm summer day, like those near the compound. He guided me to bring to mind each detail of the meadow, the feel of the grass, its thriving greenness, the soft breeze, the sun on my face, the familiar smell of the mountain air and plant life. Then he counted backward slowly from ten, each number bringing me away from his office and into the meadow.

That first time, we didn't try to bring up any memories. He just got me comfortable with being in that relaxed state. It's impossible to overemphasize how important that feeling of being safe and in control was to me. I could not have done therapy without it. Because you are so powerless and helpless during a traumatic experience, you need control and safety in order for treatment to help.

I think this is why so many traumatized people become control freaks and get so angry when things don't go their way. The feeling of loss of control recalls the traumatic memories. We try to correct that by taking control of as much of our environment as possible. This can be hard on everyone around us, as my wife and I both know well. To this day I still struggle to see that when I get angry over things like a messy house, I need to step back and realize that the urgency I feel is not related to my current life but to my past. Later, I would work on managing my anger and learning to back off when I had these reactions. Just like my dad had done at the VA.

When I came out of that first session, Jody could see that I was relieved by how it had gone. I knew that the nightmares wouldn't stop right away and that I had a lot of work to do, but the feeling that I would inevitably end up like Clayne began to ease.

In our second session, Dr. Bill hypnotized me again, first bringing me to my safe place in the mountains as he counted backward from ten. Then came the hard part. He had me recall one of my painful nightmares about Warren. He didn't want me to start with the most terrifying experience, just with one that haunted me frequently. After I was relaxed, he told me to bring to mind as many details of the memory as I could recall. He asked me to focus on the pain I had, where it was located, and the sensations I had felt at the time.

I started with the first dreams, where I'd seen not much more than Warren's hand, pulling me down a hallway. I tried to make myself think hard about what I'd felt. And then suddenly, I was back there. Warren was taking me by the hand, out of that basement classroom into the long dark hallway. I could see the wood paneling around me, feel the metallic taste of terror in my mouth. Now my heart was pounding and my throat was dry. I was five years old. It was going to happen again and I couldn't stop it. No one was going to help me—or even notice my pain. It nearly overwhelmed me with the physical symptoms and visceral sensations of fear.

But Dr. Bill quickly brought me back to the meadow with slow, deep breathing. He reassured me that I was safe now, and that I was no longer that terrified little boy. His deep voice—so real and so different from Warren's saccharine sweetness—was my anchor. He was there for

me. He had me think about the calm of the meadow and told me to try
to bring that same sense of relaxation back with me while I thought
about Warren and the hallway. He wanted me to try to be in both places
at once, as best I could.

Dr. Bill had explained to me how traumatic memories are different.
With most memories, the emotion involved is just a faint echo of what
you felt at the time. You remember a basic story of what happened and
whether it was good or bad. But traumatic memories aren't like that.
The emotion is the memory, and when something brings up that past,
you feel all of it again, like instant replay.

I had blocked off large parts of myself to prevent this from happening. In fact, when I started therapy, I hadn't allowed myself to think
much about any aspect of my childhood at all. What I recalled was frag-
ments—and putting them in context and in order took effort. Unless
something broke through my defenses, most of my childhood stayed behind those thick gray walls.

But it took a lot of mental energy to keep it all back there, and
Clayne's death and the events surrounding it had shattered my barriers.
I was too exhausted to rebuild them. If I tried to, I felt like I'd have to
use every ounce of willpower that I had to do so—leaving none at all to
get me through work or to be there for anyone.

The goal of the hypnosis was to allow me to recall the trauma while
in a state of calm. This would defuse the emotional power it had over
me by disconnecting the symptoms of the emotions—like the taste of
fear and the rapid heart rate—from my story.

And as the other emotions came back—particularly the shame and
sense of responsibility—Dr. Bill kept reminding me to have sympathy
for the child I'd been. He told me over and over that it wasn't my fault.
I had been a little tiny kid, practically a baby. I wasn't the adult who had
moral responsibility. I was innocent. What I'd been told was wrong.
The person to blame was Warren—not the five-year-old. This was not
God's will for me—it was Warren's perversity. And my family had done
the best they could, given the difficulty of having four often conflicting
parents raising twenty kids.

Dr. Bill had me picture how small a kindergartner is and think
about how helpless a child is when he is so young. He had me think of
my younger brothers and nieces and nephews and whether I would

blame them if—God forbid—something like that had happened to them at that age. He told me repeatedly that I was not responsible for what had happened and that it did not mean that I was bad or wrong or deserved to be treated that way. No one did.

I wept. Tears ran silently down my face every session. Whenever it got to be too much, Dr. Bill always returned me to my peaceful mountain meadow, not allowing me to experience any more of the memories than I could take at one time. My first few sessions were a blur of emotion, tears, and a growing sense of hope and relief. By starting slowly, Dr. Bill allowed me to move forward much faster than I would have done if I'd felt as though he was trying to "make" me better. I felt like he was working with me, not "fixing me," and I think that was an important part of why it worked.

As I continued therapy, I learned more and more. We were trying to take the emotional charge out of my past, to make it more like normal memory and less like flashbacks where I was out of control and back in the trauma and powerless. This would be aided by repetition—by going back over the same scenarios over and over, they would begin to lose their sting.

It's like when you see the same movie repeatedly: it doesn't move you the way it did the first time. Even if it's a great film, enough repetition will eventually make it boring. Or, at least, you will never have the same experience of it that you did at first. That's what we were trying to do to my memories—tame them so that I could move on. They might never make it all the way to "boring," but just getting to a place where they didn't disturb my sleep would make a huge difference to me.

You might think that the nightmares themselves would provide this repetition and numbing effect, and that eventually I wouldn't find them so frightening, since I had them so often and woke up safe in bed. But it doesn't work that way. When I reexperienced my memories in my dreams, it seemed to get worse with time, not better. I was caught up in the emotions every night. I couldn't help it. There was very little thought or story, just feelings and smells and sounds and images. They were disconnected, disordered.

I didn't realize until after I woke up that I was dreaming and that it wasn't happening again—*now*. The physical sensations of fear and pain made my traumatic memories feel like new experiences. To protect my-self, I'd split them off and my brain had kept them in a raw, unprocessed state. Because I'd been so young, I hadn't even had the words to under-stand and make sense of these memories at the time.

When I returned to them under hypnosis, however, I could defuse my feelings by breathing and with Dr. Bill's calming presence and guid-ance. He tied me to the present. He kept me from losing myself in the strong emotion of the past, and helped me replace the fear and terror with a new sense of power and safety.

Dr. Bill also used imagery to help me master my memories. After I'd recalled an experience and felt it fully in my safe place, he'd have me imagine putting the memory in a box, putting that box into a big black bag, and burning it in a fire. By picturing this step by step, I could make it seem real. That helped give the image power to burn away the mem-ories. I sometimes had to do this many times with the same memory be-fore it started to recede—but over time, it worked.

After the memory had been consumed by fire, Dr. Bill would have me leave that meadow and go to another one. There we would work on recalling positive memories of childhood, to strengthen them and imbue them with greater emotional power. This would also help reduce the power of the traumatic experience. I would often think of those fishing trips with Dad and my brothers, of the times we were contented, lying on the trampoline at night or of other fun times with extended family and friends.

These techniques may sound too straightforward and simple to be effective—and they certainly don't help if you do them just once, or do them without enough support. Part of what had happened to Clayne was that everything had been brought out too quickly, when he was al-ready very vulnerable because he was withdrawing from drugs. He hadn't been able to get the support and control over the process that he needed.

But if you do hypnosis with visualization repeatedly—and do it at your own pace with a skilled therapist who knows how to make you feel safe and will bring you back if it becomes overwhelming—it can be ex-tremely helpful. I think Dr. Bill made a huge difference. Although when I first entered therapy with him the nightmares got worse, over time they declined. I stopped dreading going to bed. I hated having to go back to my past, but I began to see that if I didn't, I would be stuck there forever.

Every week, I'd go into Dr. Bill's office, lie down on the couch, and count down to that trance state. The memories would come and I'd live them again. Soon, though, what was most troubling was not my memories, but my rage. Once I stopped blaming myself, it was uncontainable.

My anger became overpowering, often completely beyond my control. It wasn't fair what had happened to me. I wanted vengeance. At first, I was angry with everyone and everything. I punched walls. I yelled at my mother, my brothers, everyone around me. I snapped and shouted at Jody all the time. It got so bad that we broke up several times. I was at the mercy of my temper—and I had years of rage stored in it.

But with a great deal of effort, I eventually learned what triggered my outbursts. Dr. Bill taught me to step back and take a breath—the things that sound so easy but are really hard to actually do. Now, when I feel my anger rising, I force myself to say in as nice a voice as possible that I need ten minutes and can't talk anymore. I disengage from the situation and come back only after I have been able to calm down. I remind myself what matters and what doesn't. I tell myself that this is just a remnant of my past and that I don't want to let it affect my future. I breathe. And when I know I can be reasonable, I come back.

Now I sometimes dream about burning boxes filled with dark and evil things, but that is a lot better than the other nightmares.

TWENTY-SIX

Lost Boys Speak Out

I watched the press conference on TV. About six dozen lost boys had gathered on the steps of the state capitol in Salt Lake to bring their case to the media and the public. It was July 31, 2004. Dan Fischer had organized the event, and many kids that I knew came to tell their stories. Richard Gilbert talked about how, when he was sixteen, he had been excommunicated for wanting to stay in public school when Warren ordered everyone in Short Creek homeschooled.

Tom Steed discussed being expelled at fifteen for watching *Charlie's Angels*. Davis Holm, seventeen, told the media about having been run out of Colorado City at gunpoint by Warren's followers and living under highway overpasses afterward.[1] Later media coverage revealed that some lost boys had even become prostitutes in Las Vegas.

Dan told the forest of microphones and cameras that the lost boys needed "America's help" and that "Too many children have been exploited, victimized and discarded [by the FLDS]."

Utah's attorney general Mark Shurtleff said, "It breaks my heart and keeps me awake at night to know there are hundreds of boys and women who are abused and mistreated in the name of religion." He added that he was seeking ways to hold the church legally accountable. Author Jon Krakauer, who had written the best-selling *Under the Banner of Heaven*, about two murders committed in the name of Mormon fundamentalism (though by people who were not in the FLDS), was there to lend his support.

The press conference—and my lawsuit, which had been filed several days earlier—created a media frenzy, but my lawyers prevented me from attending major events. They said they were worried about my safety.

No one knew whether Warren would send someone to threaten or even kill me. This was a serious risk. He had begun preaching about "blood atonement." Blood atonement is an old Mormon doctrine not practiced by the mainstream church. It claims that some sins are so serious that they can only be atoned for by being killed by a member of the priesthood.

Brigham Young said in an 1856 sermon, "There are sins that men commit for which they cannot receive forgiveness in this world, or in that which is to come, and if they had their eyes open to see their true condition, they would be perfectly willing to have their blood spilt upon the ground . . . [to] atone for their sins." He said that this is done by the priesthood "to save them, not to destroy them."[2]

Accusing the prophet of sex crimes would likely count as this kind of a sin in the eyes of the FLDS. With the fundamentalists' muddy definition of consent, Warren could almost certainly justify killing someone like me to "save" me, even if I didn't want to be saved.

Warren had already proved that there were church members willing to violate the law for him. It happened all the time with the local police and with various forms of fraud, or bleeding the beast. For example, 33 percent of the people living in Short Creek received food stamps in 1998. That's more than five times the state averages for Arizona and Utah.[3] These payments were intended for single mothers—and although they were probably needed to feed all the many children these families had, it wasn't legal because the women who received them in Colorado City and Hildale were not truly single.

Colorado City also received $1.2 million from the federal government to pave the streets and provide other services and $2.8 million to build an airport, which was mainly used by Grandfather and Warren to land their Learjet.[4] Such money is not supposed to go to communities that are run by religious organizations, since that violates the separation of church and state. But the leaders of Short Creek answered only to the prophet. The story of the Colorado City public schools is long and complicated—but millions of dollars are believed to have been diverted from the education system into the church. Some school district money was even spent to buy an airplane.

In addition, there were many instances of defense contracts going to companies owned by FLDS members. These companies gave a proportion of their profits to the church and used unpaid or underpaid labor by church members, some of whom were underage. For example, in 2008, the *Miami Herald* reported that a company formerly known as Western Precision received $1.2 million from the federal government for parts for military planes.[5] From my own experience having worked when I was fourteen on construction projects and in a factory, I knew these practices were widespread, and other former members have sworn affidavits regarding their work for Western Precision.

Of course, Warren had shown that church members were willing to go further than just violating financial laws. Many would give up their wives and children at his command. There were loyalists willing to die for him—and it was not improbable to believe that some would kill for him.

In fact, there had been two sets of murders that had occurred in the name of blood atonement at the command of people who believed they were polygamous prophets. Ervil LeBaron—sometimes called the Mormon Manson—is believed to have ordered the killings of some twenty-five people, starting in the 1970s. He had thirteen wives and fifty children. Some of his wives and followers are known to have killed his brother and another polygamous prophet called Rulon Allred, as well as two others. Even after LeBaron was imprisoned, the killings didn't stop. When he died, he left a hit list of victims for his kids to murder, some of whom they killed. Other people on that list are still in hiding.[6] And, in 1984—as chronicled in Krakauer's book—fundamentalists and brothers Ron and Don Lafferty killed a woman and her baby under the spell of a "revelation" in keeping with this doctrine.[7]

I didn't think Warren would really go that far, but I started looking over my shoulder.

———————

Final preparations for filing the lawsuit coincided with the planning of my wedding. I had proposed to Jody in October 2003. We were getting married in July 2004. After all that she had seen me through, I knew she was the woman I wanted to marry. And I could see that she'd make a great mom.

I had always wanted a child, maybe two—certainly not twenty! I needed to be there for each child's important moments. I had seen how having a huge family made that impossible. That had sometimes made me nervous about the whole idea. But with Jody, I started to feel like having a kid was a much more realistic possibility for me.

One other thing was for sure: I definitely didn't want more than one wife. Watching what my family had gone through was more than enough to put me off that idea forever.

When I'd proposed to Jody, we were lying on her bed at her mom's house watching TV. I had been thinking about doing it for a while. So I rolled off the bed, got down on one knee, and started telling her how much she meant to me. I said that she'd been my support and my pillar through it all, that we were soulmates. Then I said, "I would love to grow old with you. Will you marry me?"

I could see immediately how happy I had made her. She said "Yes, of course" and started crying. After she'd composed herself a bit, she jokingly asked where the ring was. I said I thought she'd want to choose it—I sure had no idea what to get—so we went to the mall the next day.

My parents' lives were beginning to fall into shape around this time. After they'd left the compound, both Mom and Felicia had gotten their own homes. Dad had continued to alternate his time between her family and ours, but Felicia continuously pressured my father to make a choice. Outside of the church, she was determined not to share her husband. In 2003, Dad moved in with her, leaving Mom heartbroken.

While Mom no longer believed in fundamentalism, she still believed deeply in God. She also still adored my dad, even though he had chosen to be with her sister. She prayed every day for an answer about their future. She didn't get the sense that the door was closed. She still felt deeply connected to him. And after Dad had been gone for a few months, she says she felt God guiding her to pick up the telephone to call him. She got him at work.

"This can't be over," she told him.

And he said, "You mean you would forgive me for what I've done?"

"I've already forgiven you," Mom replied. Dad was thunderstruck. He told her that he'd decided to leave that day for California because things had not been working out with Felicia. He knew that he wanted to go back to Mom, but he'd been afraid that even asking would be disrespectful. And that was that. I was glad to see them back together for my wedding.

Jody's father paid for the nuptials and fortunately I didn't have to do much of the planning. In fact, the only thing I chose was the napkins. They were white with a silver flower and lettering saying "Brent and Jody" and our wedding date.

We were married on July 10, on the patio of a golf course clubhouse. Behind us you could see the river, and farther away the mountains. Jody wore a traditional white dress, strapless with a long train. I couldn't believe I was really marrying her when I saw how beautiful she looked. We'd moved in together a month before, and we had a local honeymoon in Park City, Utah. We couldn't take more time to go farther.

Two weeks later, the attorneys filed my lawsuit against Warren. A month after that, they filed the case for the other lost boys. Although the church's lawyer issued a written statement to the press denying my charges in the "strongest possible terms" and saying they were part of a "continuing effort by enemies of the church to defame it and its institutions,"[8] the FLDS took no action in court. We waited and waited, expecting a legal counterattack.

Warren was not seen again publicly as a free man.

TWENTY-SEVEN

Idolatry

Warren had officially announced that he was "president, prophet, seer, and revelator" of the FLDS church on August 5, 2003. By that time, all of his followers who had previously lived in Salt Lake—including most of my father's family—had moved to Short Creek to await the end of the world.

Warren had already begun cracking down on the people of Short Creek: canceling the 2003 celebration of Leroy Johnson's birthday in June and the Pioneer Day Parade in July, which commemorates the date that Mormons first settled in the Salt Lake valley. On August 10, 2003, Warren preached a sermon painting himself as Moses and his people as worshippers of the golden calf.

This is what led up to it. July 26, 2003, was the fiftieth anniversary of a government raid on polygamists in Short Creek. The people of Short Creek—led by the Barlow family, which had traditionally held more power in Colorado City and Hildale than the Jeffs—had erected a monument to honor the suffering of the families involved.

The 1953 raid went awry in many of the same ways that the raid on the FLDS compound in Texas did in 2008. Dozens of families were split. Back then, the Arizona National Guard, state police, and sheriffs swooped into town, expecting to surprise the residents. But church members had been tipped off and calmly awaited the police, singing hymns and patriotic songs—at the instruction of Uncle Roy.[1]

All of the men present were arrested, and 43 mothers and 263 children were removed from Colorado City. The children were made wards of the state, but unlike in 2008, they were allowed to live with their mothers away from the community. For two years, the families remained separated until a judge ordered them reunited in 1955. The raid had been extremely politically unpopular—costing the Arizona governor his career.

As in Texas, it was difficult to justify taking children from their mothers for the sins of their fathers. The images of chastely dressed women and weeping toddlers were as compelling then as now. What had looked on paper like the right thing to do—change a situation that had been compared to slavery for women—didn't feel that way in practice. So the state backed down.

Uncle Roy had "declared that the deliverance of the people in 1953 was the greatest miracle of all time," according to a plaque that was placed on the monument when it was dedicated in 2008.

Defying Warren, the Barlow family—many of them descendants of prophet John Y. Barlow—had refused to cancel the dedication ceremony. And so, on August 10, Warren gave a hectoring sermon saying that God had given him a revelation about the monument.

"Verily I say unto you my servant Warren, my people have sinned a very grievous sin before me in that they have raised up monuments to man and have not glorified it to me," Warren thundered. "Reparations have to be made . . . My people, let thee repent of their idolatry."[2]

He ordered the monument destroyed. Its pieces had to be scattered in the mountains so that no one could ever find them and rebuild it. He said that the people were now unworthy of blessings. There would be no more weddings, priesthood meetings, baptisms, or services held in the meetinghouse until the people had fully atoned for their sin. Even laughter was forbidden, as it allowed the spirit of God to escape. The only blessing that was still permitted—which was, indeed, obligatory—

was tithing. Since Saturday Work Days supported the financial well-being of the church, these too were not stopped.

Life in Short Creek became even more grim. Somewhere around this time, a pit bull or rottweiler mauled a toddler to death and Warren banned all dogs from the community. Church members were required to take their pets out and shoot them. If they couldn't or wouldn't do it, Dee Jessop—the zookeeper who had slaughtered the cows in our survival class—would do it for them.

By 2004, there were only a few people between Warren and uncontested, absolute power over the FLDS. One was Fred Jessop, the bishop of Short Creek. Jessop was well into his nineties and very popular among the townspeople. I'd met him only a few times myself—once for a lecture on my wild ways when I lived there—but I knew folks trusted him as a compassionate leader.

Warren knew that if he didn't neutralize Fred, he wouldn't be able to control the Barlow men. Eighty-year-old Louis Barlow had once been considered the next prophet. If the Barlows and Fred Jessop joined forces, Warren might lose his power. But without Fred, the people would likely stay loyal to Warren. And so, suddenly, Fred disappeared.

By this point, the FLDS had outposts in Mexico, Colorado, South Dakota, and Texas. Warren had directed the purchasing of these properties. In Eldorado, Texas, the church had claimed that they planned to use the 1,691-acre property, valued at $700,000, as a "hunting retreat." Instead, they built the Yearning for Zion (YFZ) ranch, named after a hymn Warren had written. It had room for about two thousand people, including huge houses for large FLDS families.

Construction on the first-ever FLDS temple began as soon as the property was purchased. This was ominous because some say that blood atonement can be carried out only inside a temple—and there were rumors that this temple housed a furnace that could produce temperatures as high as 2700 degrees Fahrenheit, hot enough to incinerate a body so completely that there would be no way to tell who—or even what—had been burned.

The temple was another sign of apocalyptic thinking. The FLDS claimed that when the final stone of a temple is laid, the people will be "lifted up." Why this wasn't necessary for the prior preparations for "elevation" made by Rulon and Warren, I couldn't say. Perhaps Warren had decided that this was why those prior elevations hadn't occurred.

Rumors flew that Fred was being held at the YFZ ranch—or in a compound in Mexico—against his will. Others believe that Warren had him killed. Still others say he lost the will to live because he was kept away from his family and friends. He was never seen alive again.

On January 7, 2004, Warren called a meeting of the people at the Johnson meetinghouse. Again he expressed his anger and disappointment with his followers, chastising them for their faithlessness and continued sinning. He went on and on and on, condemning their disobedience and lack of respect for the priesthood.

When he had whipped everyone up into a frenzy of self-recrimination and fear, he told a group of men—including Louis Barlow, several other Barlow men, and my uncles David, Hyrum, Blaine, and Brian Jeffs—to stand up. Warren called these men "master deceivers . . . Verily, thus sayeth the Lord to this people, all those who join with these deceivers and hypocrites will be darkened and will have to be cast out." To the men's wives, he said, "All you ladies married to these men are released from them and will remove yourselves immediately from their presence. If you don't, I will have to let you go."[3]

Another thirteen or fourteen men were summarily excommunicated in the same fashion, their families "released" to more "righteous" men. My brother Aaron was assigned a new "father." My uncle David was devastated by the loss of his family.

Then Warren made a bizarre statement to the men he'd targeted. "The work of God is a benevolent dictatorship. It is not a democracy. If you go along with this, raise your right hand," he said.[4]

All of their hands went up. Turning to the assembled worshippers, Warren asked if they accepted the excommunications as the will of God as well. Every right hand in the room was raised as one, even though people were exchanging looks and clearly unsure about what to do. But when Warren asked anyone opposed to stand, no one dared. Why the hand-raising exercise was necessary if God dictated his word through the prophet was left unstated. Clearly, the new prophet had felt he needed to take the people's pulse before proceeding with so bold a power grab.

He then had his followers kneel for the next round of prayers, instructing the excommunicated, as always, to "repent at a distance" but continue their tithing until such time as he determined they were worthy of return. Warren rushed off the stage during the final amens, apparently afraid that he'd gone too far and that his people would protest. But again, no one did.[5]

Now Warren had everything he needed for his own dictatorship. When I had been sent to the principal's office as a child, I had noticed that many of his books were about Hitler. I learned later that he had extensively studied William Shirer's *The Rise and Fall of the Third Reich*, seeing the Nazi führer as his own idol. Warren even claimed that he arranged marriages to breed children with the "purest" blood, refusing to see the genetic disorders that sometimes resulted as a natural consequence of inbreeding. He said God changed people's DNA to avoid such problems in priesthood marriages—if the people were truly worthy, or something like that.

Without services and priesthood meetings to preside over and weddings to officiate at, Warren's public appearances declined. Some say that he had decided that the monument had permanently "desecrated" Colorado City and Hildale; others say he had never much cared for the area and didn't mind abandoning it. Either way, he began to avoid Short Creek. Our lawsuits had made public appearances too risky and driven him underground.

When he failed to respond to my suit, my attorneys began trying to subpoena him to answer it. They hired a private investigator, Sam Brower, who lived in southern Utah.

Brower had previously worked for Ross Chatwin, an FLDS member who had refused to vacate his home or allow his wife to be reassigned to another man. He'd defied Warren, even though Warren had the legal right to evict him.

Chatwin had held a press conference in Colorado City announcing his refusal to comply in January 2004. Brower had tangled with the local police several times during his work for him, and they were clearly still under Warren's control. Now the investigator spent months in and around the border towns, trying to learn where the prophet was staying and how he was hiding.

Brower also connected with state law enforcement officials, including representatives from the attorney generals' offices in both Arizona and Utah. The lost boys press conference, our lawsuits, and related publicity had revealed the dark side of the FLDS under Warren. All of this put pressure on law enforcement to do something about the reports of underage marriages, sexual abuse, domestic violence, welfare fraud, and other crimes that were being uncovered.

But since the 1953 raid, states have been reluctant to take on polygamy directly. Back then, the much-maligned governor of Arizona who had called for the raid had identified many of the same problems found in the church today. In a radio address about it at the time, he said that investigators had found "statutory rape, adultery, bigamy, open and notorious cohabitation, contributing to the delinquency of minors, marrying the spouse of another, and an all-embracing conspiracy to commit all of these crimes, along with various instances of income tax evasion, failure to comply with Arizona's corporation laws, [and] misappropriation of school funds."[6] In other words, virtually the same crimes we were suing Warren for in my lawsuit and the lost boys' case.

Now, however, the increased attention to my story and those of the other lost boys added to prior accounts from women and girls who had fled. The media began demanding action, spurred by the outrage our stories had provoked. If they'd been allowed to hear my brother Brandon's deposition, the fury would have escalated further. But such proceedings are secret until they are used in court.

Brandon sat calmly in front of a sheer white curtain facing a video camera and a group of lawyers and their aides—and two of the men who had been involved in Warren's crimes. The only one who was missing was Warren: he was still underground. Brandon's deposition was being taken in the law offices of some colleagues of my attorneys, in order to accommodate the videotaping and the number of people present.

Brandon looked determined and purposeful, dressed in his Class A army uniform, with insignia reflecting his rank as specialist, which is the equivalent of corporal. He had already served for over two years, having joined the day after 9/11. He was giving the deposition because he was to deploy for Iraq within days for an eighteen-month tour of duty. Given the danger he faced, we didn't know when he'd next be available to give testimony, if ever. Not long before this, Brandon had told me that he had important information that could help with my case.

For legal reasons, I wasn't able to be present to support my brother as he supported me, but the video was painful to watch. My brother started out unemotional, giving clear, precise answers as Greg Hoole questioned him about his background and education and what he was taught about obedience and respect at home and in church. Brandon said that he'd been trained to "obey every word [teachers and church leaders] said, without question."

And, then, responding to Greg's continued questioning, Brandon began to tell his story. "[Warren] and some of his brothers would come and single us out and take us to the bathroom down the hall." His voice broke here as he continued. "[They would] tell us to go inside the bathroom." Brandon sobbed quietly and then went on. "He told us that what was about to happen was the will of God and part of becoming a man." At this, Brandon wept openly. "He'd take us in the bathroom and tell us, tell me, to pull down my pants and repeatedly raped me."

Greg gave Brandon some time to compose himself and then asked how old he was at the time. "Five or six, I can't remember exactly," Brandon responded. He said that it happened more than ten times, "it happened over years." My brother then discussed the roles played by Warren and his brothers in the attacks, saying that one of them—who was actually sitting directly in front of him—"was more violent than the others, more aggressive."

Brandon's bravery, dignity, and integrity were obvious in every word, even as he discussed the most difficult things. Then Greg asked him if he still has emotional and mental aftereffects. He said "Yes," and then burst into tears again.

"I don't know exactly where to start," Brandon said. "It was a total betrayal, total betrayal of trust, of everything that they said that they stood for, that they were doing God's work and they were defiling children." He added, "The only time I show any emotion is when I'm talking about this. I'm completely emotionless about everything else." His eyes showed his pain as he faced the camera.

The church's lawyer—who had already made it clear that he was not going to defend Warren in this civil case and who had tried to get out of appearing by saying that he was no longer even acting for the church—began the cross examination. He started by trying to make it look like Brandon wore his uniform as a way of seeking sympathy or projecting authority.

"Are you on duty today?" he asked. Brandon explained that under military law a soldier must wear a Class A uniform while he is in the service if he appears in a court proceeding. From there on out, it was clear that no line of questioning—even about the details and timing—would undermine Brandon's truth. His body language became hostile as he faced his attackers, but Brandon remained unshakable.

A truer act of brotherhood would be hard to find. I remain grateful to this day and awed by my big brother's courage. Brandon considered filing his own suit too, but he couldn't because, due to his age, the statute of limitations for him to file abuse charges had run out.

After taking the deposition, my lawyers were chomping at the bit to get Warren into a courtroom to face us. They could see that it was these so-called "saints" who were defiled, not the children they had devastated. But Warren remained among the missing.

TWENTY-EIGHT

The Decision

The Hoole law firm is located in an old pioneer house near downtown Salt Lake City. The small conference room we were in had a big picture window, with rippled leaded glass and French doors. I sat around a conference table with Dan Fischer, Greg Hoole and his brother Roger, and the six other lost boys in the lawsuit. It was early 2005, and we faced a decision about our legal strategy, one that most people would find extremely difficult.

Law enforcement officials were still unable to serve Warren with papers. He had remained underground, supported by church members. He frequently bought new luxury cars—BMWs, Suburbans, and other SUVs—to slip around the intermountain West, where he had scattered his wives. Occasionally, he conducted plural weddings. Rumor had it that he had 180 wives by this point—many of them formerly my grandfather's.

Warren had apparently fired his lawyer. He had told his people to "Answer them nothing" if required to appear in court or respond to the media. The phrase comes from the Book of Mormon. In the relevant passage, two true believers are brought before judges and tortured; they do not respond to their unjust captors and the corrupt legal system.[1] In our modern legal system, this response was a risky tactical mistake.

Our attorneys explained that, as trustee of the United Effort Plan, Warren had certain legal obligations. These were determined by law in the papers that created the trust. Consequently, if any trustee failed in such duties, the state had the right to take over a trust to protect its members. Because of the legal nature of the trust, this can be done despite religious objections.

At this time, the UEP was valued at $110 million. But it was land-rich and cash-poor. By failing to respond to our subpoenas, Warren made the trust vulnerable to a default judgment in our favor. According to Greg Hoole, this could give each one of us "seven figures"—or at least a million dollars.

To collect that money, however, property in Short Creek would have to be sold. And this had the potential to force some of my family and the families of the other lost boys out of their homes. If we wanted money, it would come at a price to them.

Alternatively, we could ask the Utah attorney general to have a judge appoint a new trustee. Doing this would mean forgoing a near certainty of getting large sums of money for ourselves. The first responsibility of any new trustee would be to fight us in court to protect the trust's money. In essence, if we took this path, we'd be fighting to protect the trust from ourselves!

Nonetheless, appointing a trustee would not only prevent the court from liquidating the trust to pay settlements to us, it would also keep Warren from legally evicting families from their homes at his whim. The trustee's official task would be to manage the trust to benefit the people whose money and property made up the United Effort Plan.

So our choice was a clear one. Take the money for ourselves to punish Warren and, as a result, probably hurt our families who were still in the church, potentially rendering them homeless. Or, use our lawsuits to push the state to appoint a trustee.

For me, it was not a difficult decision. My main goal had always been to bring Warren to justice, not to get money. Sure, it would be nice to be a millionaire. I did have fleeting thoughts about a Ferrari and a big house for Jody. But I wouldn't have been able to enjoy my wealth know-ing that I'd gotten it by punishing my family. And Warren wouldn't be affected much at all if we went after money, since he could still collect tithing.

Of course, some family members would hate us for going against the prophet, no matter how we did it—but there was nothing we could do about that.

Greg had called me before the meeting to ascertain how I felt, and I told him plainly that I wasn't in it for the money. My friend Richie agreed.

But later, as Richie looked around the small conference room, he thought he saw some doubts on the faces of one or two young men. When Joanne Suder had led the legal team, there had been lots of talk about how rich we were all going to be soon. Some guys were obviously furious with their families for having thrown them out. After a minute, Richie stood up and wrote a favorite quote of his on the whiteboard. It said, "What you do for yourself dies with you when you leave this world, what you do for others lives on forever." Then we wrote our votes down on a piece of paper, folded them up, and handed them to the lawyers.

But it turned out that Richie didn't need to worry. Our vote was unanimous. We would take on Warren, not go after the trust's money. We all maintained our commitment to rejecting the money, even when the lawyers talked to us privately. Afterward, we all went on a ski and snowboarding trip.

Greg told me later, "We approached it very carefully because we didn't want the boys influencing one another; we wanted everyone to make their own decision. They all seemed very certain to me that they were not interested in the money. Now I'm sure there's been times when paying their bills that they think 'I shouldn't have done that,' but I don't know. My brother and I were just flat out impressed by their commit-ment to try to do something that would be more helpful and more ben-eficial to the families, even though they would be despised for it."

From our perspective, we hoped that in the long run the families in the church would understand that we'd been trying to protect them.

TWENTY-NINE

Most Wanted

As 2005 turned into 2006, Warren remained underground. We later learned that he dressed like a Gentile in casual clothes, adding baseball caps and wigs to complete his disguise. He traveled frequently, never staying in one place for long. He visited the capitals of all forty-eight contiguous states, intent on performing a ritual to call down "the wrath of God." At each capital building, he shook "the dust off his feet in condemnation." According to the Bible, Jesus did this in places that rejected him, and Mormon scripture says it leaves "a cursing instead of a blessing." Warren also had intimate visits with his favorite wives. Then he preached fiery sermons to the occupants of each "safe house" about the imminent coming of Christ and the presence of the devil in the world around them.

He hectored his wives and the families with whom they lived, saying they had to repent or they would soon perish in the apocalypse. When one man he'd entrusted with a few wives got arrested for driving drunk, Warren reassigned this man's own wife and kids before he was able to return home. The guy came back to an empty house and had no way to find his missing family.

Our lawyers, meanwhile, had contacted the attorney generals of Utah and Arizona, offering to help in the criminal prosecution of Warren. They pushed the state of Utah to seek an administrator to oversee the UEP. The UEP was clearly now in default of its fiduciary duty: it wasn't protecting the members' assets from our legal attacks.

In early 2005, Judge Denise Lindberg began considering the cases. The attorney generals were worried that the church would sell off its assets to generate cash while it could, before a trustee could take over. There was evidence that this was exactly what the church was doing, dismantling some equipment in preparation for sale. But another judge issued a restraining order preventing the church leadership from liquidating the trust in any way.

In June 2005, the courts acted, appointing Bruce Wisan, an accountant from Salt Lake City, to oversee the UEP. We had won our first victory. Warren could no longer legally force church members to leave their homes. He might still say they had to go, but the courts would not uphold his evictions. I was overjoyed. True, Warren wasn't in prison yet, but he'd lost his main source of financial power and a key point of leverage.

Warren, however, was still nowhere to be found. I talked to people at the Utah attorney general's office about filing a criminal case against him, but even with the evidence we had from Clayne, Brandon, and me, prosecuting decades-old sexual abuse is extremely difficult. They wanted a much more recent victim.

"They want a slam dunk," my lawyer told me. "Law enforcement is particularly sensitive in bringing cases against the FLDS. They want to pursue only cases they think they have no chance of losing. That said, I'm disappointed they didn't bring a case, as I thought the evidence, including the corroborating evidence, was compelling."

Arizona attorney general Terry Goddard agreed, telling the *Arizona Republic* after I filed my case, "Of everything that's happened, the lawsuit could be the most important development . . . Our biggest problem has been getting credible victims to come forward, and my understanding is this young man is extremely credible."[1] But it wasn't up to him to file criminal charges in Utah.

After failing to file charges in my case, prosecutors had a problem. No one else was willing to come forward. People who had left the church remained terrified of Warren's power, and no one in the church would do anything. We all knew that Warren was still committing sex crimes against children, most obviously marrying underage girls. But without a specific victim's testimony, they were not going to file criminal charges.

At first, law enforcement officials were stuck. All their leads came up dry. Girls who had left the FLDS refused to press charges. Boys who had been abused by Warren had the same issues that my brothers and I had regarding the time that had elapsed. Boys also lacked the matrimonial proof that the girls who were forced into underage marriages had. For girls, there were ceremonies involving parental knowledge and permission that marked their initiation into sex with older men. Brower and others kept looking for more possible cases.

Finally, county investigators in Arizona convinced a young woman who'd left the FLDS to press criminal charges. She'd been forcibly married at sixteen, becoming the second wife of a twenty-eight-year-old man with four children.[2]

Arizona prosecutors planned to charge Warren as an "accomplice to rape." They would charge the young woman's husband with committing the rape. The victim hoped to remain anonymous so that her family wouldn't find out and try to talk her out of prosecuting the prophet.

Unfortunately, her grand jury testimony was leaked to the media and her name rapidly became public. As she'd feared, her family pressured her to drop the charges. She was afraid of losing them and so she dropped the case—and disappeared from public view.

It was frustrating. Without criminal charges against Warren, not much effort would be made to capture him. A judge had ordered Warren to respond to our suits in 2004. Police chase criminals—they rarely track down those sought only in civil cases. Warren could potentially dodge our suits for years. With a trustee running the UEP, Warren did have much less power, but as long as he was a free man, I did not feel that justice was being served. And there was nothing I could do about that if the prosecutors wouldn't take my case.

But luckily, Utah investigators then found a young woman named Elissa Wall, who had an even worse story than their prior underage victim. Warren had forced her to marry her first cousin, whom she hated. She was just fourteen at the time. She'd complained directly to Warren about not wanting her husband to have marital relations with her.

For months, Elissa too did not want to press charges. She had heard what had happened to the other woman. She was pregnant, in a new relationship, and wanted to get on with her life. However, after numerous discussions, she did finally agree to prosecute. At first, she insisted on using a pseudonym: "MJ." This made everything much more difficult. Finally, charges were filed in Washington County, Utah, on April 6, 2006. Elissa's privacy was strictly guarded.

At long last, a criminal warrant was issued for Warren's arrest. Elissa would eventually agree to go public—and her criminal charges kicked the manhunt into high gear.[3]

Since we'd filed our suit, Sam Brower had spent thousands of hours and traveled hundreds of thousands of miles searching for Warren. He was so outraged after talking with us that the hunt became a personal quest. He talked to apostates who gave him scraps of information gleaned from families still inside the church. He hung out in Hildale and Colorado City. He dug through boring property documents and did hundreds of tedious Internet searches.

At one point, he discovered an FLDS compound in Mancos, Colorado, where he suspected the prophet had spent some time. Before he could get there, a reporter accidentally alerted the owners. The journalist had been caught taking photos and the compound was rapidly abandoned. Another time, Brower visited the Eldorado compound. He believes Warren was probably inside at the time, but he couldn't get to him.

And so for many more months, Warren remained beyond the reach of the law. Then, on October 28, 2005, Warren's brother Seth was arrested in a bizarre incident in Colorado. He was weaving between lanes on the interstate, about two hours south of Denver. Another driver reported to police that a Ford Excursion was being driven erratically. Cops expected a typical DWI arrest.

However, when they pulled Seth's vehicle over, they learned otherwise. The second man in the car was Seth's nephew, Nathaniel Steed

Allred. Allred claimed that he'd been paid by his uncle for "sexual services." Apparently, it was the delivery of those services that caused Seth's concentration on his driving to slip.[4] As I later said to Larry King, he had been caught with his pants down.

The police found $142,000 in cash, some illegal drugs, $7,000 worth of prepaid credit cards, and seven no-contract, untraceable cell phones—along with printouts of some of Warren's sermons and sealed envelopes addressed to "Warren Jeffs" or just "the Prophet." Seth claimed he didn't know where Warren was but also boasted that if he did know, he wouldn't tell the police anyway.

Among Warren's correspondence was a letter from the Short Creek police chief that declared both his and his fellow officers' allegiance to Warren. "I hope to hear any directives you have for me," it said in part.[5] This would be invaluable evidence in our quest to end the law enforcement careers of Colorado City police who obeyed Warren rather than the law.

The arrest reenergized our search. But it wasn't until May 6, 2006, that the most important break in the case came. The FBI put Warren on its "10 Most Wanted" list.

My dad and I were asked to appear on the *America's Most Wanted* TV show to talk about why Warren needed to be tried and convicted. There were now two skinny, six-foot-plus religious fundamentalist polygamists on the FBI's list: Warren and Osama bin Laden. One hundred thousand dollars was offered for information leading to Warren's arrest.

Jody and I lived in a two-bedroom apartment at this time, with furniture we'd found at a moving sale as well as some salvaged from my old place. The *Most Wanted* television crew had pretty much trashed our living room, moving everything around to get the shots that they needed. Jody came home from work when they were taping and was startled to see everything so out of place when I was usually so particular about keeping everything neat.

I had been nervous about appearing on TV, but by this point I was getting used to it. I spoke plainly and simply about what had happened to me and some of my brothers. That was all most people needed to hear to make up their minds about Warren.

My father was interviewed for the program as well. *America's Most Wanted* includes reenactments. In this show, an actor playing Warren is seen seizing power from his father and threatening a little girl with implications of hellfire if she tells anyone he abused her. It was not very realistic, but it got the point across.

Once Warren was placed on the wanted list and the show aired, I was put under FBI protection. The violent history of Mormon fundamentalism combined with the nature of the charges that I'd made and the link between blood atonement and the building of a temple made them believe that I was at serious risk.

I shrugged it off, telling Larry King several days later that I didn't think Warren would really send anyone after me because doing so would only intensify the search. But it was sobering to know that at one of the last services he preached, one thousand people stood up when he asked who was willing to die for him. That made me appreciate the FBI agents whose car was parked somewhere on my street.

The media attention intensified. I did dozens of television and print interviews with journalists from around the world: Anderson Cooper and Larry King on CNN, Montel Williams, Fox News, Greta Van Susteren, Britain's Channel 4, network morning shows, and virtually all the Salt Lake media, as well as many others. Dan Fischer hired someone just to deal with the media when the lost boys became a cause célèbre. The pressure to catch Warren was also ratcheted up. Sightings of the prophet were reported everywhere.

Still, for almost all of the summer, all the rumors and tips didn't lead anywhere. The prophet had been underground for more than a year, and his followers were now claiming he could materialize and dematerialize at will to avoid his captors. God would protect him, they said. In his tapes or letters to the people, he even claimed that the 2004 tsunami that killed hundreds of thousands of people in Indonesia was God's vengeance on his persecutors.

THIRTY

A Prophet in Purgatory

On the evening of August 26, 2006, Nevada state trooper Eddie Dutchover was patrolling I-15, which leads out of Las Vegas. Around 9 p.m., he spotted a red Cadillac Escalade driving north. The luxury SUV was fresh off the lot, a 2007 model so new that it had only temporary license plates. The rear license plate was hidden in its holder, making it unreadable. Seeing the violation, Dutchover pulled the vehicle over.[1]

The officer could see that the driver had a global positioning system and a radar detector. There were two passengers in the backseat: a young woman and an extremely anxious-looking man. Dutchover sensed something fishy, drug dealing perhaps. The skinny nervous guy certainly looked as if he could be on coke or meth. The trooper began questioning the driver, soon learning that his name was Issac Steed Jeffs.

Not realizing that this was Warren Jeffs's brother, Dutchover became more suspicious when he discovered that the driver's license was from Utah but the car was registered in Iowa and had a temporary Colorado plate.

When asked his name, the man in the back seat said, "It doesn't matter." Dutchover decided to run the car and its occupants through the system. He could see that the guy in the back was practically shitting himself: the veins in his neck were visible, pulsing. He was trying to eat a salad but not seeming to get anything down.

Dutchover was frustrated to find the central computer down. He wasn't sure what to do. He could let the driver and his shady-looking passengers go—it was only a minor violation, after all. But he felt like there was something else going on. He asked for permission to search for drugs and weapons and called for backup.

Soon, the police found some $60,000 in cash, more than a dozen cell phones, two iPods, and many letters to "the president" and "WSJ." There were three wigs: blond, black, and brunette. Four laptops. A briefcase holding a Bible, the Book of Mormon, and some other religious books. Lists of addresses and phone numbers. The officers called the FBI.[2]

An agent arrived and again asked the man in the back, "What's your name?"

He looked up in resignation and said, "Warren Steed Jeffs."

The rogue prophet—the man who had done so much harm to me and my family—had finally been captured. The preacher who had banned the color red had been caught in a big red car. The man who had made women wear long underwear under long pants under dresses in Utah's heat and prohibited shorts and short sleeves and T-shirts was wearing baggy army-green shorts and a T-shirt. The woman with him was one of his favorite wives, thirty-one-year-old Naiomie, a daughter of Merrill Jessop, the man who runs the YFZ ranch. She was scantily dressed, too—at least for a church member.

———

My father called to tell me the news. At first, I didn't believe it because there had been so many unconfirmed rumors. But when I called my lawyers, they said the same thing. And when I saw Warren on TV in handcuffs, I realized he had finally been captured.

And it felt great. Now Warren would know what it was like to be powerless. I knew he was a monster, but now the world would know as well.

With Warren in jail, his reign of fear would end.

I admit I went out and got drunk that night with a friend—and I enjoyed it, too!

By now, it was clear to me how Warren had turned the FLDS from a strange religion into a dangerous cult. The difference is this: whereas a religion may have weird beliefs and practices, a dangerous cult uses a combination of seemingly innocuous techniques to control people. It usually has a charismatic leader who is seen as the source of all wisdom and salvation. Such groups can actually push normal people to do bizarre things that they would never dream of doing on their own.

By themselves, none of the techniques that Warren used to control church members are particularly powerful. In isolation, they wouldn't spur parents to abandon their spouses or children or leave their sons on the side of the highway. But taken together, cult techniques can genuinely reduce people's abilities to make healthy choices. Keeping members isolated from outside influences, keeping them too busy to think, preaching fear and terror, everything starts to add up. Getting family members to spy on one another, using police to enforce religious rulings, continually stressing that outsiders are evil—this pushes things further.

When you own people's property, control their children's education, and preach that their only road to salvation comes through obedience to you, you reduce their independence further. On top of that, if you place young girls into marriages with older men and ensure that they have many children quickly, you create whole families that can be manipulated.

Add to this the fact that the people involved have overwhelmingly lived in an underground, illegal lifestyle for generations without knowing much about other ways of life and have been subjected to endless hours of repetitive, hypnotic preaching with an emphasis on conformity, and you have a recipe for disaster. The FLDS has always taught obedience and respect for the prophet, but when it shifted to one-man rule, it lost any checks on the prophet's power.

When Grandfather took over, he was given absolute control over church members' lives. Before Uncle Roy died, Rulon seems to have genuinely believed the prophet would live forever. As far as I can tell, he didn't plot to take over the way his son did. When Uncle Roy passed, Rulon couldn't believe that his leader had not lived to see the end times with him. He took charge. But Grandfather was an accountant and was far more comfortable with numbers and rules than with people.

When Rulon became prophet he was also already weak and vulnerable to the machinations of his ambitious wife Merilyn and her protégé Warren. Warren had grown up the favorite child of a favorite wife with no experience other than that privilege and with little real contact with the outside world. He had been corrupted by seeking power and being shielded from all consequences long before he ever got it.

I don't know what made him into a pervert, but many, perhaps most, people like him were abused themselves at some point. As an abuse survivor, I myself can't understand how anyone could take the experience that I had and want to inflict it on someone else. But I do know that it happens. I don't think someone like Warren just wakes up one day and decides to do it. It has to come from somewhere.

As I look back, it seems like all his preaching about never being naked and always covering all exposed skin and avoiding the opposite sex—even making sure you are quick about changing diapers—must have been about his own struggles with his desires and his lack of control over them. When such a man becomes the leader of a group trained to be obedient, that group can be shaped by his pathology. And the FLDS was.

The closed, patriarchal leadership that he helped to shape enabled him to continue his abuse with impunity. I don't know if polygamy always produces abuse of women and children, but from my experience, it frequently does. I think it's fair to say that it always has the potential to do so in any closed system that has leadership with unchecked power. When women are seen as second-class citizens, I don't think polygamy can be anything but abusive.

With Warren in jail—held in the aptly named Purgatory penitentiary—the church could change. I know from being a lost boy how hard it is to go from being so rule bound and constricted to the wild freedom of life outside. I know how scary it is and how tempting it is to go back and just let someone else make all the decisions. But I also know how much better it can be to live as your own person, even though the transition can be terrifying. I hoped that with Warren locked up, my relatives and friends who were still in the church might glimpse freedom—and move toward it.

THIRTY-ONE

New Life

Jody had been in labor for twenty-four hours when the doctors finally decided to do a C-section. I was with her, holding her hand, trying to help but feeling pretty helpless. She was wracked with pain, but her labor hadn't progressed.

We had waited three years after getting married before she convinced me that we were ready to have a child. I had wanted to own a house, have a good job, and feel secure in our relationship first. Most of all, I wanted to be sure that I'd be ready to be a good father. Dad hadn't learned about his PTSD until most of his children were grown. I wanted to make sure that I was ready to face the challenge of raising a child with mine. When we started trying, I decided I was as ready as I would ever be.

After suffering a late miscarriage, Jody had gotten pregnant and made it through those scary early months. From her sonogram, we'd learned that she was carrying a girl. We looked at a bunch of baby name books and decided to name her Hailee.

Now I was in the operating room, masked and gloved as the surgeon began to cut Jody open. It was surreal. I watched in awe as I saw him pull my daughter out. She started crying right away—the most beautiful sound I'd ever heard. The nurses took Hailee away to clean her off and weigh her. Then they handed her to me. She weighed nearly nine pounds and was twenty-two inches long: it was no surprise that Jody had needed a C-section.

Hailee was perfect. My life flashed in front of my eyes as I held her, thinking about what had brought me to this moment. Tears welled up. I felt proud and in awe of my wife and happy and terrified. I couldn't get over the beauty of Hailee's pink, pearl-like toes and tiny, curving fingers. I was completely overwhelmed. I suddenly realized I was responsible for this little person forever. I felt a surge of love like nothing I'd ever experienced. I knew I would do anything to protect her, to ensure no harm ever came to her.

I was also hit by a wave of sadness that two of my brothers would never get to share my joy. A year earlier, I'd had a 4 a.m. phone call that was like a flashback to Clayne's death. This time, it was Dave's wife on the phone, crying. She'd found Dave's body on the couch: he'd overdosed on methadone, some other painkillers, and alcohol. Big D, the center of our family, was gone.

Jody and I had rushed over. As with Clayne, I just couldn't believe that my brother was dead. But when I saw the paramedics outside, I knew. We tried to console Dave's wife and began calling my brothers and sisters.

We'll never know if he meant to kill himself or if it was just a tragic mistake. The night before, Dave and his wife and Jody and I had had dinner with my parents. It had seemed like a perfectly ordinary dinner, but Dave did make a strange remark about wanting to have bagpipes play at his funeral. When we said good-bye that night, he seemed to hug everyone a bit longer and tighter and say "I love you" with a bit more intensity than usual.

I don't know if he said that because he was planning to commit suicide or because he had some sense that his time was near. All I know is that I miss him and Clayne and so wish that they could have been there to greet Hailee.

In the waiting room, Mom and Dad were anxious to meet their

grandchild. My sister Linda and Jody's mom and stepfather were there, too. After Jody held Hailee and we took a picture, the nurses let me carry her out through the swinging doors of the operating room to greet the waiting grandparents. I was so proud.

I wasn't lost anymore, I knew exactly what my purpose was now. I had stood up to Warren, and had helped bring him to justice. Though I wished it had been my case that was heading to trial and that would soon end in his conviction, I knew that the lost boys and I had begun the process that would ultimately take him down.

It was our lawsuits that had taken away control of the $110 million UEP. Our suits also kick-started the process of decertifying the Colorado City and Hildale police, stopping them from acting as Warren's enforcers and making it easier for abused women or children to leave.

We settled with the trust, each receiving a three-acre plot of undeveloped land near Colorado City and establishing a $250,000 Lost Boys Assistance and Education Fund, to help boys who had left or would leave to get on their feet and continue their schooling. I felt good about that.

And shortly before Hailee was born, Warren apparently confessed to being a sex offender during a prison visit with his brother. In prison, people like Warren who are charged with sex crimes against children are seen as the lowest of the low. They are held in solitary confinement for their own protection—as they are targeted for rape and assault.

Warren began fasting in his twenty-three hours of daily solitude and spent so much time on his knees praying that he developed sores. Already thin, he lost twenty pounds and became skeletal and shaky. During a videotaped prison visit in January 2007, he told his brother Nephi that he was a "wicked man." He confessed that he had molested one of his sisters and a daughter. As a result, he said, he really hadn't held the priesthood keys at all since he was twenty. "I am not the prophet," he said. "I never was the prophet, and I have been deceived by the powers of evil."

He said that God had visited him in his cell "to test and detect me and He saw that I would rather defy Him than obey Him because of the weaknesses of my flesh . . . I yearn for everyone's forgiveness for my aspiring and selfish way of life, in deceiving the elect, breaking the new and everlasting covenant and being the most wicked man on the face of the earth."

Several days after this confession, he tried to hang himself. He was taken to the hospital, given a psychiatric examination, and returned to prison. Two days later, he began throwing himself at the walls, saying he was trying to achieve blood atonement. All he got were bruises.

He told his brother that he wanted the word of his failure as a prophet spread even to apostates and Gentiles. At a court hearing, he held up a piece of paper that said "I am not the prophet."

And with the criminal case under way, it seemed clear that Warren would probably never leave prison alive. Although he hadn't confessed to all of his crimes, I felt that as long as he was locked up, justice had been done.

Looking at my new baby, I knew I faced lots of sleepless nights and had lots to learn. I felt a rush of compassion for my parents, thinking about all they'd had to juggle with so many children and about how hard life had been in the church. I was glad I had only one wife and child to worry about. I still don't know how my parents got through it.

But I was also glad that Hailee would grow up surrounded by our family. True, it was more complicated than most, but that wasn't what mattered. There were so many important things they had taught me that I wanted to share with her. Both Mom and Dad looked so proud as I came through those doors. With the love I felt at that moment, we could face anything together.

Epilogue

WARREN JEFFS

On November 7, 2007, Warren Jeffs was sentenced to two consecutive terms of five years–to–life, after being convicted of two counts of being an accomplice to the rape of Elissa Wall. That means he will serve at least ten years in prison on those charges alone.

He is currently facing additional charges of sexual conduct with a minor and incest in Arizona, and may also face similar charges in Texas in relation to his own marriages to girls aged twelve and fourteen.

FLDS IN TEXAS

On April 3, 2008, Texas officials raided the Yearning for Zion ranch, the FLDS compound in Eldorado, where Warren had ordered a temple built. Based on information received in a telephone cry for help—which now appears to have been a hoax—they removed over four hundred children on suspicion of child abuse and underage marriage.[1]

Texas child welfare officials flew me in so that I could testify about sexual abuse in the FLDS, but they decided instead to have me brief experts who would be working with the FLDS children. Although most of the children have now been returned to their parents, and the media has portrayed the raid as an overreaction by child welfare officials, twelve people have been indicted so far for being involved in forced underage marriages.[2]

FLDS IN COLORADO CITY/HILDALE

With Warren in prison, life in Colorado City and Hildale has improved. Although it is still a very closed society, there is much more contact between church members and relatives who have left, including lost boys. Laughter, music, books, and dogs have returned and people no longer face the threat of having their families and homes reassigned.

Warren's most fervent followers now live at YFZ ranch in Texas—and they are at highest risk for child abuse and future underage marriages because their world is still so limited. The future of the FLDS as a whole is still murky: a new leader could unify the people in either positive or negative ways, the group could splinter, or attrition could set in, leading to a slow decay.

LOST BOYS

My brothers and I who were lost boys illustrate many of the risks faced by young men who leave the church, who now number in the hundreds. New boys also continue to leave. In our case, six of us left the church as teenagers to live on our own. We were luckier than some in that we were not always completely cut off emotionally from both of our parents—but like the others, we did not have their financial support or close guidance when we left.

Only one of us had completed high school before leaving—and that was at Alta Academy. While almost everyone eventually got GEDs or finished high school later, only one of us—Brandon—has gone to college. Many of us have struggled with alcohol and other drug problems. Two of my brothers became addicted to heroin and similar drugs, one had a period of methamphetamine addiction, and I certainly smoked more than my fair share of marijuana. Many of us have suffered depression and half have some symptoms of or meet the full criteria for post-traumatic stress disorder.

And of course, I have lost two big brothers: Clayne and David, whom I still miss every day. Although we do not know whether David's overdose was intentional, his addiction was clearly influenced by what happened to him in the church and the way he left it. Without therapy and the support of the people around me, I might well have joined them.

The rest of us have now managed to build lives for ourselves. I am married and chasing Hailee as she becomes a toddler, and I am working for Ultradent. My brothers are mostly married or engaged and everyone is working. But, as is true in our case, the level of severe drug and mental health problems among lost boys is much, much higher than for other young men of the same age.

For those interested in learning more and in helping the lost boys, this is the contact information for the Diversity Foundation:

Shannon Price, Director
505 West 10200 South
South Jordan, Utah 84095
Office: 801-553-4556
Fax: 801-553-4600
http://www.smilefordiversity.org/

Acknowledgments

BRENT JEFFS

I would like to first of all wholeheartedly thank my wife, Jody, for all the support she has given me throughout all of this. Second, I want to thank Mom and Dad for their love and for always believing in me. In addition, I thank all of my brothers and sisters, but especially my brother Brandon, whom I admire in so many ways for his strength and determination.

Without Dr. Bruce Perry, this book would never have been possible. I also thank our agent, Andrew Stuart, and editors Phyllis Grann and Jackie Montalvo, all of whom truly enhanced our work in many ways. Dr. Dan Fischer and Shannon Price at the Diversity Foundation provided important support, as did my attorney Greg Hoole. And of course, last but not least, my awesome, talented, and gifted writer Maia Szalavitz.

MAIA SZALAVITZ

Much thanks to Peter McDermott for everything, as always. Echoing thanks to Diversity and to our incredible agent, Andrew Stuart, and superb editors Phyllis Grann and Jackie Montalvo. Many thanks to Lisa Rae Coleman, my friend and transcriber. Special thanks to Alissa Quart for her friendship and illumination and to the "Matildas," especially Deborah Siegel and Rachel Lehmann-Haupt. And particular gratitude to Dr. Bruce Perry for introducing me to Brent. Brent, it has been a joy and an honor to work with you and your family, and I thank you all for your dedication, courage, and kindness in sharing your story.

Notes

CHAPTER 1

1. Brodie, Fawn, *No Man Knows My History: The Life of Joseph Smith* (New York: Vintage, 1995), 294.
2. Ibid., 340.
3. Doctrine and Covenants, Sec. 132.
4. Brodie, *No Man Knows My History*, 300.
5. http://journalofdiscourses.org/Vol_11/refJDvol11-41.html.
6. Bistline, Benjamin G., *Colorado City Polygamists: An Inside Look for the Outsider* (Scottsdale, AZ: Agreka Books, 2004), 20.
7. Ibid., 21.
8. Ibid., 21.
9. Zoellner, Tom, "Rulon Jeffs: Patriarch, President, Prophet for Polygamy," *Salt Lake Tribune*, June 28, 1998.
10. Ibid.

CHAPTER 2

1. Hollenhorst, John, "Birth Defect Is Plaguing Children in FLDS Towns," *Deseret News*, February 8, 2006, http://www.deseretnews.com/article/1,5143,635182923,00.html?pg=1.

CHAPTER 4

1. Langford, Terri, "Court Ends Monitoring of Most FLDS Kids, but 37 Children Still Under Watch as Investigations of Abuse Continue," *Houston Chronicle*, October 30, 2008, http://www.chron.com/disp/story.mpl/headline /metro/6087268.html. Note: There have been various numbers given because some girls originally believed to be "children" were, in fact, adults. This seems to be the most accurate.

CHAPTER 6

1. Sermon of Rulon Jeffs, January 24, 1988, reprinted in Alta Academy yearbook, 1994.
2. Ibid.
3. Ibid.
4. Sermon of Rulon Jeffs, December 4, 1992, Alta Academy Devotional, reprinted in Alta Academy yearbook, 1993.

CHAPTER 15

1. Warren Jeffs Dictation, July 27, 2006, available online here, originally cited by *Houston Chronicle*, http://www.childbrides.org/Warrens_underage _mariages_dictation.pdf.

CHAPTER 20

1. Singular, Stephen, *When Men Become Gods* (New York: St. Martin's, 2008), 69.
2. Bistline, *Colorado City Polygamists*, 193.
3. Ibid.
4. Winslow, Ben, "Judge May Decide Fate of FLDS Trust Today," *Deseret Morning News*, August 14, 2006.

CHAPTER 26

1. Adams, Brooke, "Polygamy's Lost Boys Need Not Walk Alone," *Salt Lake Tribune*, August 1, 2004.
2. Scheeres, Julia, "Killing for God," Trutv.com accessed October 2, 2008, http://www.trutv.com/library/crime/notorious_murders/classics/ervil_lebaron _cult/6.html.
3. Zoellner, Tom, "Polygamy on the Dole: Welfare Aids the Illegal Lifestyle of Many Families in Utah-Arizona Border Community," *Salt Lake Tribune*, June 28, 1998.

4. Ibid.
5. Douglas, Jack J. R., "Polygamist Sect Received Taxpayer Cash," *Miami Herald*, April 13, 2008.
6. Scheeres, "Killing for God."
7. Krakauer, Jon, *Under the Banner of Heaven* (New York: Doubleday, 2003).
8. Manson, Pamela, "Leader of FLDS Named in Abuse Suit. Allegations: The Polygamous Church President, Two Others Are Accused of Sexual Assault," *Salt Lake Tribune*, July 30, 2004.

CHAPTER 27

1. Bistline, *Colorado City Polygamists*, 58–61.
2. Ibid., 195.
3. Wall, Elissa, *Stolen Innocence* (New York: HarperCollins, 2009), 284–86.
4. Ibid.
5. Ibid.
6. Howard Pyle, radio address, July 26, 1953.

CHAPTER 28

1. Alma, 14:17 http://scriptures.lds.org/en/alma/14/17b.

CHAPTER 29

1. Reaves, Joseph, "Troubles Dogging Polygamy Prophet," *Arizona Republic*, August 1, 2004.
2. Wall, *Stolen Innocence*, 345–46.
3. Ibid., 352.
4. http://www.austinchronicle.com/gyrobase/Issue/story?oid=oid:388481.
5. Singular, *When Men Become Gods*, 175.

CHAPTER 30

1. Singular, *When Men Become Gods*, 202–5; also, various news accounts.
2. Ibid.

EPILOGUE

1. Blumenthal, Ralph, "Court Says Texas Illegally Seized Sect's Children," *New York Times*, May 23, 2008.
2. Langford, Terri, "8 More Indictments Issued in FLDS Polygamist Case," *Houston Chronicle*, November 12, 2008.

Photo Credits

All insert photos are courtesy of the author, except:

Page 7, top: Tiffanie Mar
Page 7, bottom: PictureMe Portrait Studios
Page 8, top: Tom Green County District Court photo archives
Page 8, bottom: Jud Burkett/Pool